Goodbye Shanghai

a memoir

Sam Moshinsky

REAL
FILM AND PUBLISHING

First published in Australia in 2009. Re-published in 2016 by Real Film and Publishing ABN 93978529400 www.realfp.com.au

National Library of Australia
Cataloguing-in-Publication entry:

Author: Moshinsky, Sam, 1934-
Title: Goodbye Shanghai : a memoir / Sam Moshinsky.
Edition: 1st ed.
ISBN: 978-0-9875179-6-8

     Moshinsky, Sam, 1934-
     Jews, Russian-China-Shanghai-Biography.
     Jews, Russian-China-Shanghai-History.
     Shanghai (China)-History-20th century.
     Shanghai (China)-Biography.

305.8924095113

p 51   -Image of Rabbinical students in a Hongkew Lane, reproduced courtesy of Horst Eisfelder
p 67   -Image of Pearl Harbour, Hawaii, 7th December 1941 © Newspix / News Ltd
p 83   -Image of section of the Ward Road Heim in Hongkew c. 1940, photographer Stefan D Konig, reproduced courtesy of Rachel Konig
p 107 -Image of Emperor Hirohito © Newspix / News Ltd
p 113 -Image of dancing man at end of World War Two - © Newspix / News Ltd
p 197 -Image of the Bund, reproduced courtesy of Stan Fookes

Edited by Romy Moshinsky and Deborah Blashki-Marks
Cover design and book design by Jacki Starr @ Starr Design

To Danita, Jamie, Amira, Joey, Tommy, Hannah,
Sonny & Mia Moshinsky with love.

Dear Grandchildren,

I am constantly aware of the contrast between my childhood in Shanghai and your life here in Melbourne. It was incredibly different in terms of colour, taste, language and landscape, but those years were also shaped by wider forces. My early life spanned an extraordinary period of history, when the upheavals of the world affected everyone in unimaginable ways.

Over the years, I have been urged to write about my life in the exotic city of Shanghai. Although I was always attracted by the idea, there were more pressing concerns including my studies and later, my career, starting a family and doing community work. With your arrival, in fairly rapid succession, I finally found the impetus and opportunity to put pen to paper.

Watching you all grow up, and as our relationships develop, I am reminded of the special bond I once enjoyed with my grandparents, whose unstinting love and care ensured that I always felt secure and happy. You probably think, as I did, that grandparents are born old. In actual fact, my story will reveal that I too was once young and spirited. I hope that you will come to know how much I gained from exposure to so many cultures and to inspiring people, who taught me values that would guide me through life.

And so my grandchildren, I thank you for motivating me to embark on this story-telling adventure.

With all my love

Grandpa Sam

I was relieved when dawn finally broke on the morning of the 25th September 1951, the date of my departure from Shanghai. I hadn't slept well that night, as the reality of my impending journey finally took hold of my nerves. I had been out of Shanghai on only a few occasions in all my seventeen years: to Japan with my grandparents as a young boy and, holidaying with my family after the war, in the nearby mountain resort of Moganshan. Now I would be travelling on my own as a vanguard of the family, to far-off Australia to start a whole new life. I was already exhausted from the hectic and demanding pace of the previous few weeks, dealing with the seemingly endless formalities of obtaining exit and entry visas. There had been the difficult task of disposing of possessions, many of them of sentimental value, which I could not take with me, as well as the sad farewells to life-long friends who were still waiting for their papers to come through.

Saying goodbye to Tonia, our Russian head servant, and our Chinese cook, both of whom I had known for the better part of my life was not easy. Nor was it easy to bid farewell to Wang Tu Tsai, the manager of our Shanghai Cardboard Box Factory who had known me since infancy. I had already said goodbye to the Brothers at St Xavier's and St Joan of Arc's who were busily turning over their schools to the new education authorities, prior to their own enforced departures from Shanghai.

The hardest part was, of course, the final parting from my own family, especially my grandmother. I knew that she would miss me terribly as, since my grandfather passed away, I had become the central element of her existence. At her age, she must have wondered whether she would ever live to see me again.

With a heavy heart, I left the Doumer Apartments, certain that I would never see the building again. We made our way through the streets that I had come to know so well, to the railroad station where I was to board the train to Canton. A number of family friends were also making the same journey and my father had arranged for them to keep an eye on me until Hong Kong, where another set of friends, the Godkins, would take over.

Promptly at noon, the train began its departure. Martial music began to play over the station's loudspeaker system and soldiers stood at attention, as a train pulling out of a station was then considered a special event. My luggage had already been loaded on and, after tearful farewells, I settled into my allocated window seat in a spacious sleeper compartment. The trip to Canton was to take three days, with an overnight stay there, before travelling to the border crossing into Hong Kong.

The journey turned out to be uneventful and even boring. We were discouraged from moving around too much as, at short notice, we would have to return to our compartments when we were about to approach an important locality. Bridges, in particular, were treated as militarily sensitive and when the train crossed a bridge, we were obliged to pull the shade over the window.

The family friends periodically checked on me to see if I needed anything, which I didn't. There was nobody my own age with whom I could pass the time. There was no formal entertainment provided, other than patriotic music, which was continuously piped over the loudspeaker system. Food, in the perpetually crowded restaurant car, was plentiful but plain and monotonous. Card playing and mah-jong were ways to pass the time, but I played neither of them.

Reading was, therefore, my only option over the next three days. The books I had brought for the journey were by my favourite authors, Somerset Maugham and Upton Sinclair. But despite the fact that I was finally on my way, I was still too unsettled in my mind to concentrate on the words. In any event, the continuous blaring of Chinese music was very distracting.

I spent a large part of the trip sitting by the window, gazing at the passing scenery of endless tiny fields and toiling Chinese peasants. Strangely, I found it calming to reflect on Shanghai and the impact my life there had made on me as a person.

When I was born, Shanghai was the most unique city in the world. A cosmopolitan and modern western enclave, in China but ruled by European traders, totally dedicated to the pursuit of commercial gain. It was a magnet to fortune seekers and a refuge to the oppressed. The city I was now leaving was the exact antithesis: firmly governed by a new breed of authoritarian Chinese rulers totally committed to a communist philosophy and the eradication of the humiliation inflicted by past European masters.

During the first seventeen years of my life, I experienced wars, changing regimes, different currencies and a variety of schools that reflected the evolving political landscape. In a world obsessed with conflicting nationalism, my family survived as stateless residents, neither subject to, nor the responsibility of, any country. We were instead, largely sustained by our Russian Jewish culture and community and the benign indifference of local authorities. Amidst grinding poverty we lived a life of plenty and comfort. And even when my life could have been one of personal unhappiness, following the divorce of my parents when I was very young, I was lucky enough to have had a family which shielded me from pain and lavished me with much love and attention.

Grandfather holding me on the steps of the factory

1

MY ARRIVAL

'The North China Daily News provides a glimpse of Shanghai's vibrant commercial life on the day of my birth....Tucked away in the political sections, however, the newspaper also reveals the political fragility of the world into which I was born.'
Sam

The 3rd of July 1934 dawned hot and sultry. It was the height of summer and Shanghai had been experiencing a heat wave for some weeks. Air conditioning was enjoyed by a privileged few but most of the population was sweltering in the soaring temperatures.

On that day, in Mrs. Schwartz Maternity Ward, 22E Rue Pere Robert, in the heart of the French Concession and walking distance from my family's business and residence, I was born to Bronislava Zaslavsky and Abe (or Abrasha as he was known) Moshinsky. Both of my parents were Russian-born Jews permanently residing in Shanghai. They had been married the previous year.

My birth certificate was entered in the Register of Births kept by the Shanghai Ashkenazi Jewish Communal Association, rather than in official state records as would have been the normal practice nearly everywhere else. This provides an early clue that the city of my birth was no ordinary city. It truly was like nowhere else on earth. Effectively ruled by a small group of European merchants, Shanghai was home to several million Chinese, who possessed no political rights, as well as a polyglot of peoples seeking haven from persecution.

The *North China Daily News* provides a glimpse of Shanghai's vibrant commercial life on the day of my birth. Included are details of the many vessels arriving and departing and the various localities where cargo was to be discharged and loaded on. The paper, replete with advertisements for shipping services and places of entertainment, conveys a confident and comfortable environment. Shanghai's prosperity was unaffected by the severe worldwide economic depression.

Tucked away in the political sections, however, the newspaper also reveals the political fragility of the world into which I was born. Individuals and events that would soon engulf the world in the most terrible of conflicts were beginning to make their ominous appearances. Reference was already being made to the skirmishes between the Chinese and Japanese military forces. Japan had already invaded Manchuria, a northern province rich in resources, whetting its appetite for further encroachments on

China. In Europe, Adolf Hitler was already ensconced as Germany's chancellor, heralding potent threats to that country's Jewish community. Even in civilised England, the scourge of anti-Semitism was rearing its ugly head as the paper reported a 15,000 strong demonstration of Fascist Blackshirts led by Sir Oswald Mosley.

In the seventeen years that I lived in Shanghai, I was a beneficiary of the prosperity that my family enjoyed, but my life was also greatly affected by these global conflicts.

Grandfather and Grandmother
in Vladivostok

2

MY RUSSIAN JEWISH ORIGINS

*'Today we know the names of the founders of the
Vladivostok synagogue. We want others to know
who they are to remember them. ......Moshinsky...'*
The Federation of Russian Jewish Organisations

Growing up, I was exposed to and influenced by many different cultures - Chinese, British, French, Russian and Jewish. But of all of these, it was the Russian Jewish heritage of my father's family, which moulded me during my formative years. And so my story really starts before my birth, in the Ukraine and Siberia.

My paternal grandfather, Shlema Shimonovitch Moshinsky was born in 1884 in the small town of Kitaigorod in the Kiev Gubernia, a province in what is now the independent country of Ukraine, but was then part of the tsar's Russian Empire.

In 1903 Shlema married 17-year-old Maria Caisman from Odessa. The story of their courtship and the details of their wedding are not known to me but their marriage was followed by the birth of their only child, my father Abe, on the 14th August 1904.

Odessa, the city of my father's birth, was large and contained a sizeable and vibrant Jewish population. The city was located on the Black Sea and over the years it emerged as a major port. By Russian standards it enjoyed a temperate climate.

The Jewish presence in Odessa dates back to 1789. As it prospered, it drew Jews from all over Russia. Jews were engaged in the export and wholesale trade, banking and industry, the liberal professions and various crafts. Many prospered and, by the outbreak of World War Two, the Jewish population there had grown to 180,000, approximately 30 percent of the total population.

From the inception of the Zionist movement, Odessa became an important centre for Zionist intellectuals and activists. Fabled names such as Leo Pinsker, who wrote *Auto-Emancipation*, Ahad Ha'Am, Meir Dizengoff, a founder of Tel Aviv, Chaim Nachman Bialik, and the founder of the Revisionist (now Likud) organisation, Vladimir Jabotinsky, were all part of a heady scene. There was also a vibrant Jewish cultural life manifest in theatres and Yiddish publications. But as cultured and cosmopolitan as life was in Odessa, it did not mask the precarious and wretched existence of the approximately four million Jews who lived in the Russian empire. Under the influence of a rabidly anti-Semitic Russian Orthodox Church, life for them was extremely oppressive. The oppression ranged across the whole gamut of the Jews' existence. They were systematically excluded from all the benefits and opportunities which society offered. This involved restricted access to higher education, employment in government service and entry into a variety of occupations and professions.

Russian Jews could not live anywhere they pleased, and were herded into certain parts of the country, known as the 'Pale of Settlement'. Worse still was the practice of conscripting (press-ganging would probably be a more apt description) young Jews into the tsarist army for a 25-year stint. There they were subjected to a daily hell of miserable duties and cruel discrimination. They lost their identity and their lives were ruined.

The harshness of this existence was not limited to the Jews. The tsar's regime was incompetent and corrupt and the plight of millions of Russians and other minorities was often just as unbearable. To deflect blame and distract the general population as their sufferings welled up to shocking proportions, the government, in league with the Russian Orthodox Church, cynically resorted to identifying the Jews as the main cause of the general population's misery, thereby unleashing a series of the most brutal of pogroms.

In the Pale of Settlement, many Jews lived in small villages, in Yiddish called 'shtetls'. There they were defenceless against the sudden swooping of Russian militia, often Cossacks, who would rape, pillage and murder the vulnerable Jews. In 1903, a particularly brutal pogrom occurred in the town of Kishinev, and many Jews were killed. This sparked a mass exodus of Jews to the more civilised and liberal societies of the United States of America and Western Europe.

A number of Jews, however, deterred by the language and cultural barriers described in the letters from the first immigrants abroad, chose instead to migrate to Siberia, a huge and forbidding part of the tsar's empire. Settlement in this sparsely populated part of the empire was being actively encouraged and construction of the Trans-Siberian Railway, which was begun in 1891, greatly facilitated this.

My grandparents were amongst those who chose to go to Siberia. Vladivostok held some appeal. The fact that it was 'as far away from the tsar as possible' was an attraction. And friends who had already made the journey there had written of the opportunities and relative freedoms which this emerging city promised. And so, in 1906 with two-year-old Abe in tow, they travelled across nine time zones to the other extremity of the Russian empire.

Vladivostok principally owed its existence to the fact that it was an outlet to the Pacific Ocean, with a harbour whose waters did not freeze in winter - a critically important attribute for a year-round functioning port. The tsars had for some time colonised Siberia and were actively involved in the settling of these vast regions in the east. But access to the sea, a vital element in their governance, could not be satisfactorily carried out until an understanding could be reached with China, then in possession of the territory in which the future Vladivostok was located. Such an agreement came about in 1868.

The city's development was initially slow, due to its remoteness and harsh climate. Few Russians were prepared to make the long and arduous journey from the relative comforts of European Russia. As a result, Vladivostok had a substantial Chinese population who, very early on, perceived the opportunities posed by its location and the wealth of its hinterland. The imperatives of the settlement policy ground on regardless and by 1875 enough Russians were persuaded to settle there to form a town council, which was elected by all of the 165 Russians who possessed the right to vote.

The completion of the Trans-Siberian Railway to Vladivostok, a track of 9,288 kilometres from Moscow - a great engineering feat by any standard - opened the way for entrepreneurs and workers alike to settle in the region, which started to take off commercially. Imposing edifices, many of which are still standing, were constructed to house the headquarters of great trading families like the Skidelskys and the Brynners.

The city's growing prosperity enabled my grandfather Shlema to establish a successful business in packaging. The records in the official archives list him as an artisan and he applied his skills to perfecting a system for coating a thin film of paraffin on to cardboard and then converting this into leak proof containers. Cottage cheese and sour cream were important elements of the Russian diet and his new containers became popular for storing these products. Business flourished and the family thrived. His new-found wealth allowed Shlema to purchase a new house in a desirable part of the city and later, an even bigger home.

Grandfather was a resourceful, if not eccentric, businessman. My grandmother often told the story of how he used to hire key workers. He believed that if a man eats heartily, he works heartily. So, before employing anyone, he used to set a plate of food down to see if the worker ate it with gusto. If he did, he was hired.

As the Jewish community grew, Shlema became a founder and financial supporter of a new synagogue. Shlema's participation in the affairs of the synagogue involved him in the engagement of a remarkable religious head. Rabbi Meir Ashkenazi was born in 1890 in Tcherikov, in the Pale of Settlement, from where he fled to Harbin, in Manchuria. In 1918, he responded to the urging of Rabbi Daniel Chaskind, then the elderly Rabbi of Vladivostok to come there to help strengthen the existing community. Rabbi Ashkenazi was highly respected and revered in this new congregation.

Shlema participated in Jewish community meetings, including one to raise funds to provide matzos for the poor and another to extend the synagogue to encompass the land next to it. Unfortunately, the onset of the First World War and the Russian Revolution aborted these expansionary plans.

War and revolution not only put paid to plans for the extension of the synagogue, they also spelled the end of a very happy existence. The communist revolution heralded the end of private property and business enterprise, as well as Jewish religious life, something that had already gathered pace in European Russia. In Siberia, and particularly in far-off Vladivostok, this all took much longer. Distance was a factor, together with the ill-fated 'Intervention' by the United States and Japan, which landed troops in Vladivostok to shore up the rapidly collapsing tsarist empire and slowed down the pace of change. A short-lived establishment of a semi-independent buffer republic between Russia and China also gave hope that in this far-off territory things would be different.

It was not until the latter part of the 1920s, as communism began to consolidate itself over the whole of the former tsarist regime, that Grandfather had to accept that continuing business, as he knew it, would be impossible. Shlema and Maria realised that they would have to seek a future elsewhere. Once they came to the conclusion that they no longer had a future in Soviet-controlled Vladivostok, they carefully considered their options. Much would depend on their religious and cultural background.

The 'White Russians', who supported the now defeated tsarist regime, feared for their lives and fled. A number actually migrated to Australia, many of them settling in Brisbane. Some travelled to Harbin, which was relatively close and which already had an existing Russian community.

For the Moshinsky family, now including my father aged in his 20s, Shanghai beckoned. Their friend, Rabbi Ashkenazi, the spiritual leader of the Vladivostok Jewish community, had already settled in Shanghai in 1926 and his correspondence gave them some insight into the city and the nature of its Russian Jewish community. Also, they had to take my father Abe into account, and where his future lay. The fact that Father could speak fluent English after a year in Chicago, where he had studied and spent time with his mother's family, the Caismans, was a relevant factor. But foremost in Grandfather's mind were the commercial possibilities on offer. Shanghai offered the possibility of re-launching the packaging manufacturing business which he had been forced to abandon.

Grandmother's family in Odessa, before moving to Chicago

The two Moshinsky residences in Vladivostok

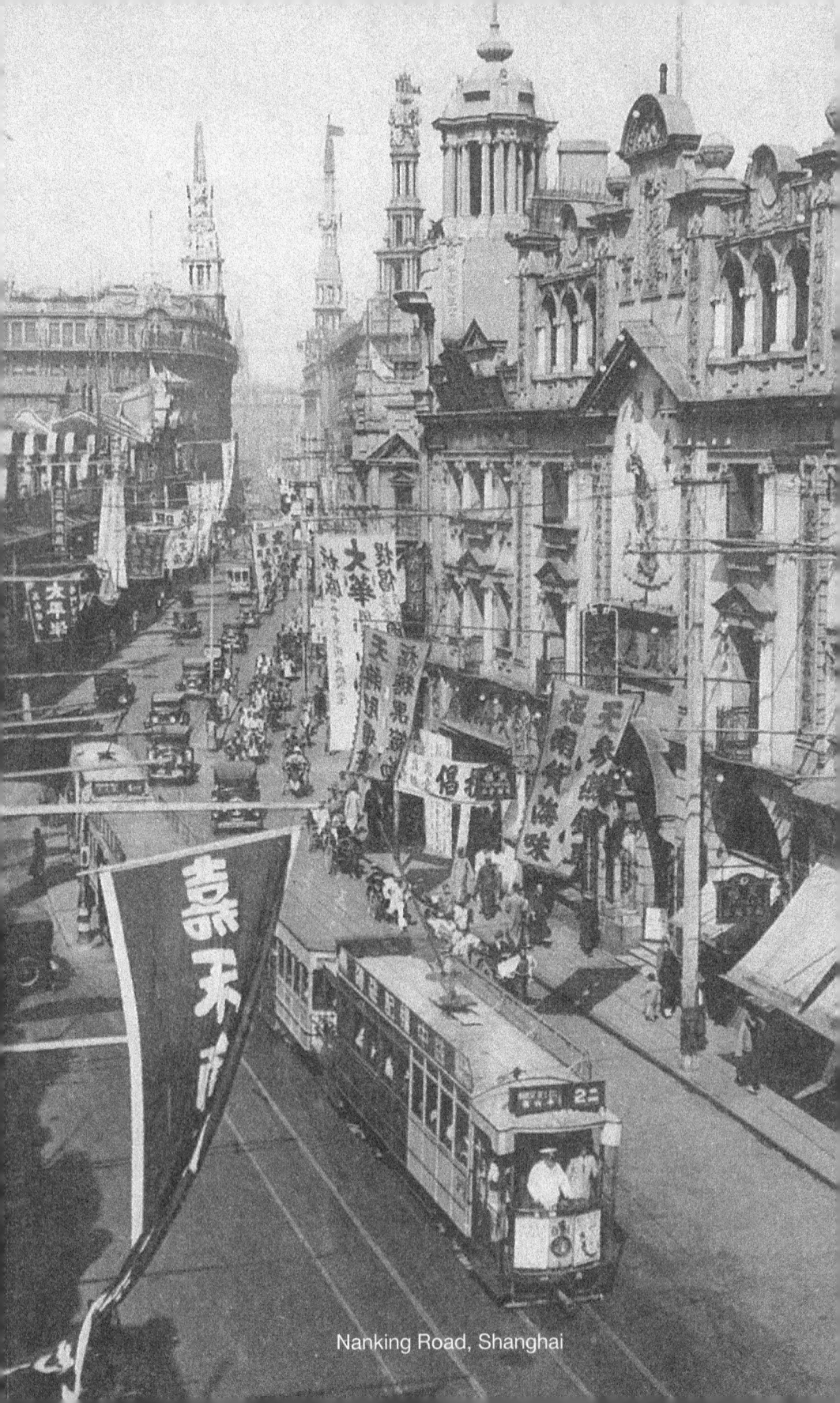

Nanking Road, Shanghai

3

SHANGHAI – TEA, OPIUM AND FOREIGN VICTORY

'There is a class of evil foreigner that makes opium
and brings it up for sale tempting fools to destroy
themselves, merely in order to reap profit.'
Lin Zehu, the Chinese High Commissioner to the
British government in 1839

By the late 1920s, Shanghai was already a city of superlatives. It was China's largest port, a leading industrial centre and its richest city. It was home to a large and diverse group of European people as well as millions of poverty-stricken Chinese from the countryside, to whom Shanghai offered both employment and physical security. Although physically part of the Chinese mainland, Shanghai had a unique political status: it was, in effect, an 'international city' because of the complicated and convoluted interplay of the various governing authorities. Entry into Shanghai was not under the sole jurisdiction of the Chinese authorities and it was easy. Those who arrived in Shanghai, usually by ship or rail, just merged into the large city and fended for themselves.

Shanghai was and remains a unique phenomenon. Geographically, it is virtually at the mouth of the Yangtze River and it acts as both the entry, as well as the exit, point for much of China, the world's most densely populated country. The saga of its emergence as an international city is a curious and important aspect of history that dates back many centuries. It is a saga that shaped my existence and the person that I am today.

By the 17th century, China's rulers already possessed an ancient and unshakable belief in their own and their nation's superiority. After all, it was the Chinese who were the first to invent the printing press, which was also used to print paper currency, as far back as the Norman Conquest. They were the ones who developed the eyeglass, were the first to exploit coal (the 'burning rocks' which Marco Polo first noticed) and they invented gunpowder. The rulers viewed China 'as a nation around which the rest of humanity centred'. The emperor was called 'the Son of Heaven' and 'Lord of 10,000 Years'. This heightened sense of superiority was accompanied by a strong disdain for all other peoples. This attitude was manifest in the demeaning and insulting manner in which foreign dignitaries were received when seeking an audience with the emperor, and also in disdain for all the products of the 'foreign devils'.

In 1664, China presented King Charles II with a gift of two pounds of some black scented leaves. Within 50 years, the British had developed an insatiable taste for Chinese tea, with enormous and increasing quantities of it being imported from China, year after year. Not only did the British people become addicted to the taste of tea, the British government likewise developed a financial addiction to it, as the exchequer levied a 100 percent tax on every pound of tea imported.

China's disdain for foreign products meant that they refused to trade the tea for British goods. Instead, China insisted that the tea be paid for in silver. In those days, silver, in the form of Spanish dollar coins, enjoyed the status of an international currency, much like the American dollar of present times. Unfortunately for the British, however, their supply of Spanish silver dried up completely during the American Revolution of 1776.

Restricting the importation of Chinese tea, in response to the shortfall in the availability of silver, was neither a political nor a financial option. The predicament for the British was indeed serious. Clearly a product had to be found which the Chinese needed as much as the British needed their tea. And that product turned out to be opium.

Opium was originally imported into China as a medicinal product, primarily to prevent diarrhoea, which was caused by dysentery, then endemic in China. Its initial suppliers were Arab traders who obtained it from Turkey via the age-old caravan routes. Later, during the 17th century, the Dutch entered this trade, sourcing opium from Bengal, in India.

Eventually the British muscled in. By 1782, they were transporting individual shipments of up to 3,000 chests from India to China. Opium's harm as an addictive drug was already known to the Chinese authorities who became increasingly alarmed at its clandestine and growing importation. So much so that in 1799 an imperial edict was issued, drawing attention to its harmful effects and condemning the drug's traffickers.

This action proved to be of no avail. While the opium trade was originally embraced to generate the silver to satisfy the British daily tea fix, a relatively mild addiction, the sheer profitability of the 'remedy' fanned the greed of the opium merchants. Neither the debilitating effects upon its users, plain for all to see in the mushrooming opium dens of China, nor the vehement opposition of a proud and sovereign empire, would serve as a restraint.

By 1816, however, when the conflict between opium traders and Chinese authorities reached a peak, Britain had become a superpower and the word 'Great' was being increasingly applied to it as a prefix. It had defeated its most formidable enemy, Napoleon Bonaparte, its navy was all-powerful and its king and people started to swell with the pride that comes with supreme military power. And yet the Chinese continued to insist on the traditional and demeaning ceremonies for foreign envoys. One of the most obnoxious was 'kowtowing' which involved a form of genuflecting when approaching the emperor, where the face of the envoy had to touch the floor, not once, but nine times!

Despite a number of earnest attempts by some British authorities to head off this looming confrontation, no meaningful discussions took place between the parties, as there were powerful traders who saw potential personal benefit in the successful outcome of a military confrontation. For its part, the Chinese were, unfortunately, mired in their own pride and an unrealistic assessment of the realities of a conflict with Great Britain. Their military was clearly no match for the British and their resort to the many futile, and often cruel, attempts at deterrence only strengthened the British determination to prevail.

The ensuing conflicts are known as the Opium Wars, which started in 1839 and did not finally end until 1860. They were initially fought over the opium trade and were ultimately to bring into China the ever-increasing quantities of British-manufactured goods. The wars paid off very handsomely for the British. Four years after the Opium Wars ended, the British supplied seven-eighths of China's imports. The initial transport of 3,000 chests of opium in 1782, which precipitated the conflict, had ballooned to 105,000 chests by 1879. The toll on the Chinese was immense. Apart from the humiliation visited upon its ruling classes, the horrifying problems of addiction pervaded the entire population. It was estimated that, at its peak, nearly 70 percent of Chinese people partook in opium. Even the Dowager Empress Cixi became an addict. Not till 1949, when Mao Tse Tung and his communist party took over the running of China, was the problem of opium addiction successfully eradicated.

The British were unforgiving and exacting in victory. The island of Hong Kong was annexed as a colony and in the final throes of the war, in an act of unbelievable destruction, even the beautiful Summer Palace of the emperors, just outside of Beijing, was vandalised. To cap it all, the British forced upon the Chinese authorities an abrogation of certain elemental rights of sovereignty. Under the Treaty of Nanking of 1843, special privileges and rights were granted to British subjects in five ports: Canton, Foochow, Amoy, Ningbo and Shanghai.

The key objectives of the treaty were to provide British citizens in these ports protection from the haughty and capricious behaviour of the Chinese authorities. The treaty granted them immunity from the operation of Chinese law and subjected them to British law instead. So, although the area covered by the ports remained under the technical sovereignty of the Chinese, in practice, the Chinese authorities possessed no jurisdiction over British subjects, nor, eventually, over citizens of other countries. This most unusual arrangement was called 'extra-territoriality' or 'extrality' for short.

To ensure the effective implementation of the objectives of extrality in Shanghai, areas outside the Chinese walled city were earmarked for administrative control by city or municipal councils, elected and run by the respective citizens of the countries then involved in trade with China. Initially, there were local authorities that covered Britain, France and the United States. Resident military personnel from these countries backed this quasi form of sovereignty. The result was a modicum of physical safety to enable the pursuit of commercial activity, including the nefarious opium trade, in an atmosphere that approximated life in the citizens' homelands.

The arrangement was initially designed to ensure the continuation of profitable trading and protection for a small enclave of British and other foreign merchants. Although the creation of the safe environment was intended to benefit the foreign traders, ironically, it was the Chinese who also became important beneficiaries of the enclave.

The humiliation dealt to the Chinese rulers as a result of their defeat in the Opium Wars, and the degrading impositions of its aftermath, resulted in considerable political turmoil in China. Civil strife afflicted thousands of ordinary and innocent people who sought refuge in the safety of these foreign enclaves or 'concessions' as they became known. Although the Chinese were denied the political benefits enjoyed by the foreigners, the increased physical safety and employment opportunities in the concessions resulted in a substantial Chinese influx.

The swelling Chinese population was initially viewed with consternation by the foreign authorities, who were powerless to stop it. But Shanghai was fast realising its true destiny as a major port and manufacturing centre. Cheap labour was required, and so the Chinese influx was soon viewed as a boon for the concessions.

The growth and prosperity of Shanghai was underpinned by a culture of unbridled dedication to the making of money. Shanghai, the centre of opium distribution, was now turning into a mecca for both Chinese refugees and a host of fortune seekers. The 500 million people who lived along the banks of the nearby Yangtze River presented enormous trading opportunities for such entrepreneurs. As a result, 20 years after the first foreigners settled there, Shanghai's population was exploding, overwhelming the relatively small municipal councils and forcing the dominant British and American zones to merge. The merger resulted in a new, more efficient, administration called the 'International Settlement', which was governed by an elected municipal council.

The French did not participate in this amalgamation. The French presence, known as the French Concession, was under the direct rule of a French consul, who, in turn, reported to the French government in Paris. There was also a Japanese settlement in the northern part of the city, known as Hongkew and areas under Chinese administration that reported to the nationalist government, based in Nangking. This bizarre state of affairs was to endure until the Japanese occupation ended in 1945, after which the various extrality arrangements were terminated and the city returned to full Chinese sovereignty.

The European-controlled civil administrations were focused on providing and maintaining a safe and liveable environment for business to prosper, largely unhampered by any notions of social responsibilities. In addition, the haphazard interplay of jurisdictions created an environment where immigration laws were virtually non-existent. This gave Shanghai its reputation as an 'international city', making it a haven for the persecuted, as well as the adventurous. The world's leading financial and trading institutions maintained a presence there amid this diverse and cosmopolitan group of people. Shanghai's population spanned cultures, races, political ideologies and, of course, religions. Temples of various eastern religions coexisted with Christian churches as well as synagogues catering to both the Sephardi and Ashkenazi branches of Judaism.

In this burgeoning metropolis, sometime early in 1930, without passports or visas, Shlema and Miriam Moshinsky, with their only son Abe, now a young man, took advantage of Shanghai's open door policy. They established themselves as another success story among the many other, newly-arrived refugees. Shlema applied his expertise in the manufacture of paraffin-coated containers, and began to enjoy early success. The quality of his manufacturing techniques, which he had developed in Vladivostok, enabled him to win the business of the leading manufacturer of packaged ice cream products, an American enterprise called Hazelwood. A factory was established in the French Concession, at 414 Rue Lafayette. Manufacturing took place over three floors and a spacious dwelling existed on the top floor, where the whole family lived for a number of years.

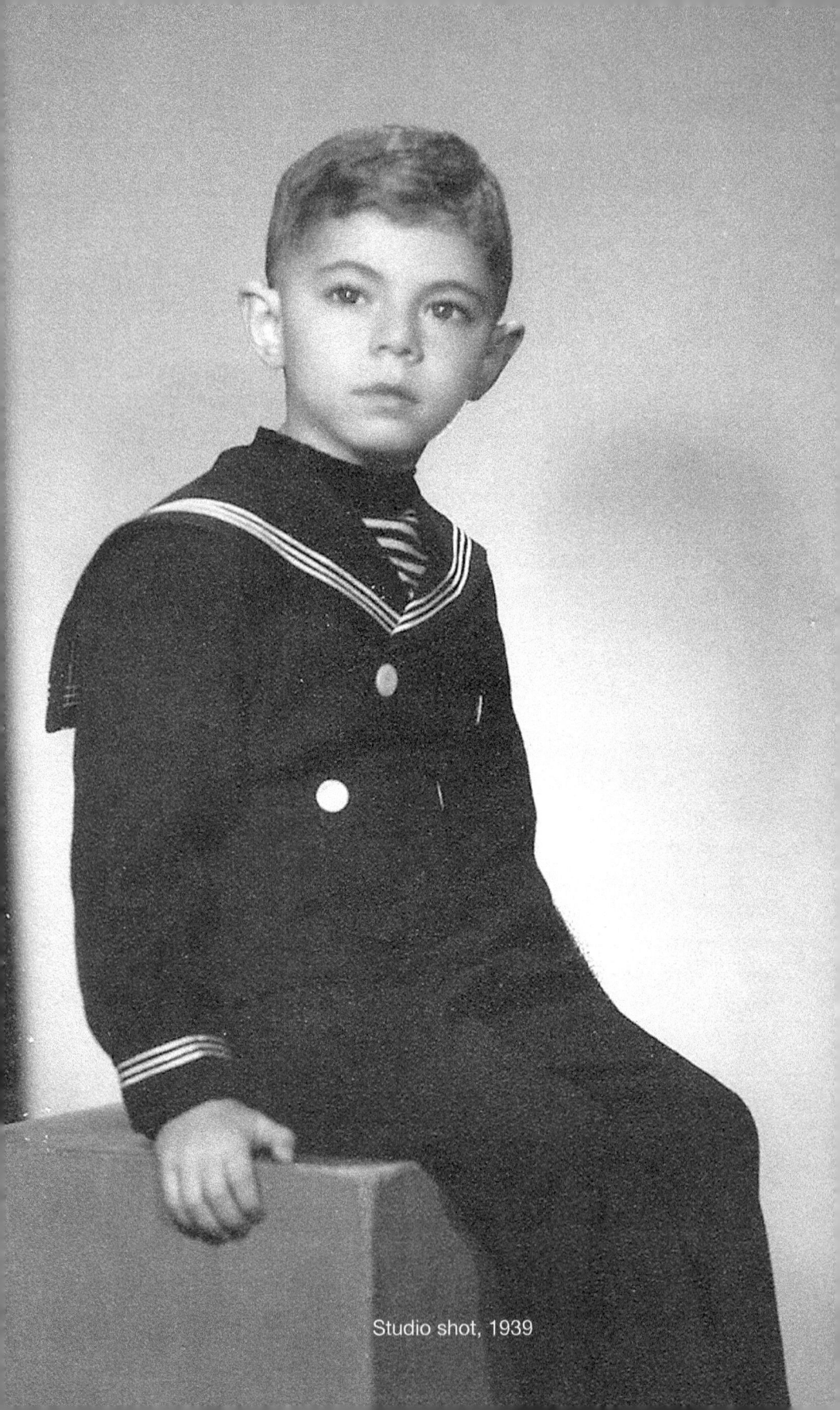

Studio shot, 1939

4

MY EARLY LIFE

*'If you develop good habits, you will not
have to rely on will power.'*
Miriam Moshinsky

On the 26th April 1933, a few months shy of his 30th birthday, my father married Bronislava Zaslavsky, aged 24, who was also born in Russia, in Genichesk, to Jewish parents. From this marriage I was born the following year. Unfortunately the marriage did not last and on the 19th February 1936, when I was less than two years old, they were divorced in accordance with Jewish law.

The Instrument of Divorce was written in Russian and, like my birth certificate, was also only registered with the Shanghai Ashkenazi Jewish Communal Association, whose religious head was Rabbi Ashkenazi, formerly of Vladivostok. The divorce settlement decreed that for the first four years of my life, my mother would take care of me. After that, reflecting the needs and cost of my education, custody would revert to my father, as he was financially best able to shoulder these responsibilities.

In practice, these terms were not adhered to. My mother came from a poor background and she soon found that she couldn't afford to look after me. So, only five months later, just before I turned two, the terms of the divorce were amended by mutual consent.

Whilst my mother retained some visiting rights, my father and his parents took over the responsibility of raising me.

I was too young to remember this period of turbulence and the circumstances of the break-up were never discussed or explained to me. Whatever happened did not seem to affect me adversely. Even though I didn't have my mother at hand, I don't remember ever suffering or experiencing distress, as everybody around me went out of their way to ensure that I was protected.

My first recollections of early life are associated with anxieties over my eating preferences and the problems they caused. As a sole parent, Father felt the need to play a decisive role in my upbringing and he believed I should eat everything placed before me. But I couldn't stomach various forms of meat, particularly types that were difficult to chew. I enjoyed vegetables, but I loathed spinach even though it was promoted by the popular cartoon character 'Popeye the Sailor Man'. I recall Father shouting at me, as he always did when he became angry, that with so many people going hungry in Shanghai, it was disgraceful (he used the Russian word 'pazor') that I should be so fussy. At times he would become particularly angry and would take off his belt and threaten to strap me if I refused to eat a particular item of food. But I was very stubborn and the confrontations would have turned ugly had Grandmother not come to the rescue. She would often sit next to me during meals, and when my father was distracted by a call, as he often seemed to be, she would swiftly snatch the offending item and eat it herself. Those early occasions were the start of a very special bond with Grandmother, which would endure until her very last days.

When it came to food and matters of health, Grandmother did much more than extricate me from a difficult time with my father. She had very defined views and standards. She personally supervised me eating at least two pieces of fruit a day. She also insisted that I go to the toilet at the same time each day and she was always around to ensure that this happened. I remember that from a very early age she would tell me that it was essential to develop good personal habits, which become second nature. She would often say, 'If you have to rely on will power, then you will fail.'

Shanghai was not a very clean place and we had to take certain special precautions to protect ourselves. A particular problem was head lice and the only solution was to shave off all my hair every year, at the onset of summer. Then I had to have my head thoroughly washed in soap, every day. Naturally I hated it. Grandmother would console me by saying that I would grow up with healthy hair. Another annual disagreeable task was de-worming. Again, because of the lack of hygiene in much of the food we ate, children, particularly, were prone to developing worms in their digestive systems. Special medicines were administered which I dreaded.

For entertainment, I would often be taken to the movies. In those days, there was, of course, no TV and no children's programs on the radio. So going to the picture theatres was very popular, particularly in summer, when they were air-conditioned. My favourite actors were the comics Laurel and Hardy, while on the adventure side, I was enamoured with Zorro, the Mexican hero who was the saviour of the oppressed. He was particularly adept at jumping on his enemies from high places, and I would try to copy him by climbing on to the top of a wardrobe and jumping down on anyone who entered the room. This used to scare people, which was the point and pleasure of the exercise. It took a couple of straps from my father and I soon stopped this practice.

I probably craved attention. Sometimes, when my hair had grown back after the annual shaves, I used to cut a square patch out, right in the middle of my head. This frightened everyone when they first caught sight of me. Grandmother used to indulge me in all this and the amah was totally helpless. But Father would have none of it, and again the strap would come out.

The amah, my Chinese nanny, was my constant companion. She was taken on as soon as I passed into the custody of my father and my grandparents, following the amendment to the conditions of my parents' divorce. In addition to my own amah, we employed a 'wash amah' who came every day to wash and iron our clothes.

My amah lived with us. She slept in the same room as me and woke me each morning. She then bathed, dressed and fed me. She would take me for walks and to visit my friends. Although we became close, I always called her 'amah', never by her name, which I cannot even recall.

The amah and I used to eat Chinese food for lunch together every day. Sometimes we had dinner together too, when Father and my grandparents were eating out at the Jewish Club or at a restaurant. Even as a toddler I was very good at using chopsticks. I could speak Chinese fluently. My first spoken language was Shanghai-dialect Chinese and, initially, my family could only communicate with me via the amah, who could speak some Russian and English. As I grew older, by mixing more with the children of my parents' friends, I acquired the ability to speak in Russian at home, as well as in English and French, the dominant European languages of the time.

As a young boy, when out walking with my amah, I was intrigued by the venerable-looking old men who sat by the road at their long trestle tables. They were scribes. China, at that time, was a country with considerable illiteracy, particularly among the many poor from the countryside who flooded into Shanghai looking for work. These illiterate people would pay the scribes to write messages to their loved ones, still living in the villages. Once these letters arrived at their destinations, the equally illiterate recipients then went to their local scribes to have the letters read out loud. That was the only form of communication available to these poor people. Some could barely afford even this form of primitive communication, adding to their hardship and loneliness.

A number of the men who approached the scribes for assistance had what we called 'pigtails'. Their hair was shaved in the front and then plaited in a long queue that hung down their back. Originally, it was a sign of submission imposed by the conquering Manchus. Some of the old men I saw also had extraordinarily long fingernails, a traditional sign of superiority, to show that they were scholars, rather than manual labourers.

I also watched with fascination, the women who hobbled down the street with their bound feet. When they were girls of only three or four years, their toes had been bent down against the soles of their feet and fastened by tightly-wound bandages that stunted their growth. It was perceived that these women endured this pain in the cause of finding a husband as this was considered alluring.

My amah would sometimes take me to see Chinese funeral processions of paper-made houses, furniture, personal items and even replicas of automobiles. The Chinese believed that these replicas, if burned on earth during the funeral, would exist in the deceased's afterlife. The accompanying loud music and exploding firecrackers always thrilled me. I also used to go with my amah to friends' birthday parties, which were always exciting. Sometimes there would be a ventriloquist to entertain us. But the best part was when a projector was wheeled out and we got to watch the latest Disney cartoons.

Very occasionally, I spent time with my mother. Once, on a birthday, the outing was a visit to an ice cream parlour. Being July, it was a very hot day and the air-conditioning in the parlour was extravagant, but very welcome. Another time, when I was seven years old, we went for a walk in a park near my new home in the Doumer Apartments. We spoke in either Russian or English, but I only vaguely remember what we talked about. I think she asked me whether I was happy, and I am sure that I assured her that I was.

What I do vividly recall about that meeting was Grandmother's attitude. She hadn't wanted me to see my mother, but it was unavoidable in terms of the divorce conditions. Shouting loudly, she made it clear to me that my mother had better not venture near our home because if she saw her, she would 'throw a bucket of dirty water over her'. This was very intimidating for me, and it created a dark cloud that hovered over me during the outing.

I think that this must have been the last time I actually saw my mother. She was not a subject to be discussed and over time it became obvious that she would have no influence over me or further involvement in my life. I must confess that I didn't long for her, nor did I feel that she represented a void in my life.

For this arrangement to succeed, Father and my grandparents indulged me with love and attention, determined that I be a normal, happy and spoilt little boy. They all gave me a special measure of care to ensure that I felt wanted, particularly Grandmother.

On the 28th March 1939, a few months before I turned five, Father re-married. His new wife was Eva Krasovitsky. She was also Russian. Her parents, Gilel and Tsiva, were extremely orthodox Jews. Like many poor Russians, they had earlier gravitated to Harbin, in the northern Chinese province of Manchuria, where they had benefited from better economic opportunities. In Harbin the Krasovitskys ran a small business selling galoshes in winter and making ice cream in summer. Eva had a very pretty sister, Nusia, with whom she was very close, and a brother Boris, who died as a young man from illness during a study trip to Russia.

Eva trained as a bookkeeper and worked for a cosmetic business. In 1938 her company sent her to work in their new Shanghai office. In the close-knit Russian Jewish social scene she soon met my father, who was a very eligible bachelor. They were married in the Russian Jewish synagogue and they moved into the spacious Moshinsky apartment on the top floor of the factory in Rue Lafayette.

I was her first challenge and she approached it wisely and with much sensitivity. Eva was determined to treat me as a son.

One memorable day, Eva took me to see a gypsy woman about my warts. For some reason, large warts started to appear on my right hand. They were extremely ugly and I was very self-conscious about them. I had bandages with all sorts of ointments covering them and I even pretended that I was left-handed, in order not to engage my right hand. Everything was tried, including a painful treatment of trying to burn these warts off, but nothing worked. The gypsy woman had rooms in a dingy building off Avenue Joffre and I was led into a crowded and foul-smelling waiting room. When I finally got to see her, she took the hand with the warts and with a pencil dipped into a dark liquid counted the warts several times. She said that they would disappear in a few days. And they did! After that seeming miracle, I was very grateful to Eva and we got along particularly well. I always looked forward to going out with Eva and Father on Sunday afternoons to the pictures. They used to spoil me with popcorn and ice cream.

Over time I started to feel that it would hurt Eva if I asked after my natural mother. As she very rarely called to see me, I stopped mentioning her or expressing a desire to contact her.

My grandparents continued to protect me from unhappiness and to involve me in their lives. For the treatment and relief of arthritis, wealthier Shanghai families used to travel by ship to Japan, to a place called Beppu, where there was an abundance of special 'curing mud'. This was done in the summer time when it was oppressively hot in Shanghai. My grandparents used to take me along, leaving my father with his new wife to run the business. I spent a lot of time with my grandparents and this was a great bonding experience.

The ships to Japan were large and comfortable. I remember that once we arrived, I found other children with whom to play. We played games wearing clothes that were distinctly militaristic, in keeping with the mood in Japan just prior to its war against the United States of America and the European powers.

In those times, the Japanese public baths had men and women using them at the same time, in an unclothed state. Naturally, Grandmother would have none of this, so Grandfather, being a forthright organiser, arranged (in other words paid) for the baths to remain open after closing time. Grandmother bathed then, by herself, while I stood guard outside the door.

I lived in the apartment over the factory with Father and Eva until 1940, when Grandfather built the Doumer Apartments. The apartment over the factory was very spacious, with a large dining room leading to a covered balcony. There was also a big kitchen, a large lounge room and several bedrooms and bathrooms. There I shared my bedroom with the amah who looked after all my needs, day and night. The rhythm of life was uneventful, but pleasant. I would often go down to the factory itself and move around the workers and talk to them in the Shanghai dialect. The various machines fascinated me and I can still recall the pervasive smells of paraffin and glue which were used in manufacturing the cardboard boxes.

I also played with the children of the key workers who lived in a row of terraced houses in a laneway behind the factory. One of them was the daughter of Wang Tu Tsai, the 'comprador' of the business. Her name was Kunka. She was very pretty and eventually became an actress in Shanghai's cinema industry. The compradors were a peculiarly Chinese institution. They basically served as intermediaries between the European owners and the Chinese workers, suppliers and government officials. Grandfather was a very progressive employer. For the key workers, he provided food and the terrace house accommodation. In this way, he ensured that the basic needs of his employees could not be gambled away or otherwise foolishly spent. He was also a very disciplined and exacting employer. At the entrance to the factory there was a huge board, on which hung the little metal emblems containing the numbers of the individual workers. Each evening, at the close of business, the departing workers removed their individual tags and then put them back in the morning when they returned. Every morning, Grandfather came down to check the board for any missing tags.

To thank us for our support, the workers always invited us to their Chinese New Year banquets. This holiday was the most important one in the Chinese calendar and the factory would remain closed on that day. The workers' wives started cooking early in the morning and I remember the bustle of activity as I wandered from terrace house to terrace house.

The eating began at midday and, in true Chinese banquet practice, there would be a continuous flow of literally dozens of dishes, well into the late afternoon. All this food was accompanied by the steady flow of warm Chinese rice-wine. I can recall Father staggering home drunk and vomiting all over the place, amid much scolding by his wife and mother. Grandfather was a more controlled drinker.

In keeping with the times, this was very much a men's affair. I remember that as I wandered around on those days, there was a lot of noise from men shouting, eating and drinking, whilst Chinese women were continuously rushing in with food and washing up.

The Shanghai Cardboard Box Factory was a successful business. It was comprised of two seasonally-oriented businesses. The main one involved the manufacturing of ice cream containers for Hazelwood. This business thrived, for the summers were long, hot and humid, and the general level of hygiene was low. As a result, it was better to buy ice cream in sealed cups, rather than in open cones, which were exposed to flies and other health hazards.

For the winter, the factory manufactured elaborate chocolate boxes. When people visited each other, it was customary to give a box of chocolates, as fruit and flowers were not easy to come by. The chocolate boxes were very popular and so the factory employed a full-time artist, a Russian man named Alexei Ryaudin, who created various pleasing designs for the box covers. I remember being told that the attractiveness of the box was even more important than the chocolates inside.

Grandfather controlled the business very strictly, continuously roaming the business premises to ensure that all was working well. Grandmother told me that he had a very basic way of controlling the level of stocks. He used to run his finger over all the stocks of paper, the mainstay of the business, to check how much dust had accumulated. Anything with too much dust had to be dealt with. Father would look after sales and relationships with the foreign customers, particularly the Hazelwood Company, because of his good command of English and his gregarious nature.

Despite the emerging conflict between Japan and China and the world economic depression, Shanghai's economy powered on. In fact, the 1930s were a time of enormous growth in Shanghai and there was a lot of building activity to show for it. Against this background, the Shanghai Cardboard Box Factory prospered and this was reflected in the fortunes of the Moshinsky family.

The amended divorce agreement

ДОГОВОР.

Шанхай, 1936 года, Июля 28-го дня. Мы, нижеподписавшиеся, русские эмигранты, Абрам Шлеймович МОШИНСКИЙ, жительствующий 414, Рю Лафайет, именуемый в дальнейшем ... и Бронислава Михайловна ..., именуемая ...

Agreement

Shanghai, 1936, 28th day of July. We, the undersigned, Russian emigrants, Abram Shleimovich MOSHINSKY, residing at 414 Rue Lafayette, hereinafter referred to as the FIRST PARTY and Bronislava Mikhailovna Moshinskaya, residing at 859 Avenue Joffre, hereinafter referred to as the SECOND PARTY, have herein come to an agreement concerning the following:

1. In accordance with the divorce agreement of 19 February 1936 concluded between the parties, the son of both parties, SAMSON, born on 3 July 1934, remained with the SECOND PARTY to be raised until he attained FOUR YEARS of age, whereupon the SECOND PARTY had undertaken to hand him over for upbringing to the FIRST PARTY.

2. Presently the SECOND PARTY has voluntarily agreed to hand over the son SAMSON to the FIRST PARTY to be raised by him from 1 August 1936 and until he attains adulthood, i.e. 21 years of age.

3. From the moment of handing over of the son SAMSON the SECOND PARTY has undertaken not to interfere in his upbringing and education as provided by the FIRST PARTY, and in general has no claims against the FIRST PARTY in connection with the handing over of the son SAMSON, either of a material or a moral nature.

4. In the event that the SECOND PARTY shall find herself in the same city in which the son of both parties Samson is resident, then the SECOND PARTY will have the right to see the same son twice a week at a time agreed to by the FIRST PARTY or his representative.

5. With the signing of this agreement, point SIX of the Divorce Agreement between both parties of 19 February 1936 will automatically be rescinded.

6. The FIRST PARTY reserves the right to revoke meetings of the SECOND PARTY with her son Samson in the event that the FIRST PARTY becomes aware of attempts by the SECOND PARTY, during meetings with the son Samson, to incite him against the FIRST PARTY.

7. This agreement ... made in THREE copies, of which one is for the FIRST PARTY, one ... and one for the office of counselor-at-law I.N.Shendrik...

(Signature – L.N.Se...
(Signature - ?)

Shanghai, 1936, 2...
B.M.Moshinskay...
agreement in the...
Registration No...

(Seal of Barrist...

7. Настоящий договор составлен в ТРЕХ экземплярах, из коих один для ПЕРВОЙ СТОРОНЫ, один для ВТОРОЙ СТОРОНЫ и один для конторы Прис. Пов. И.Н. Шендрикова.

Шанхай, 1936 года, Июля 28-го дня. Настоящим удостоверяется, что г.г. А.Ш. Мошинский и Б.М. Мошинская, в присутствии вышеуказанных свидетелей, расписались под настоящим договором собственноручно, в моем присутствии.
По реестру за № 185.

Left, top: an advertisement for the Shanghai
Cardboard Box Factory in Hongkew Jewish publication
Left, bottom: workers outside the factory
Above: The Shanghai Cardboard Box Factory

Christmas party, 1939

Above: Father and Grandfather behind their desks at the factory
Below: Wedding photo of Father and Eva. 1939
Right: In Beppu, Japan

With grandparents in Japan, 1941

REMEMBRANCE
FOR
NATURAL
SAND BATH
BEPPU JAPAN

Rabbinical students in a Hongkew Lane, 1946

5

SHANGHAI'S JEWISH HERITAGE

'Jews and Judaism have had a long history in
China, but until the beginning of the 20th century,
the existence of a 700-year-old Jewish community
in China remained almost unknown.'
John Cohen, *The Jews of China*, 2008

To most Jews, Shanghai is associated with the haven for approximately 18,000 Jews from Germany and Austria who arrived there fleeing Nazi persecution. Had it not been for the 'open door' that its unusual political status in the 1930s provided, they would have been doomed to certain death, along with millions of other Jewish people stranded in Nazi-occupied Europe.

Shanghai was also known as the home of a small but colourful Sephardi community which contributed significantly to its amazing development. There were also clusters of Eastern European Jews, such as the Russian and Polish Jews, to whom the city provided safety and commercial opportunities.

The Jewish connection with China, however, actually long preceded the arrival of these modern Jewish communities. Jewish presence in China dates back to at least the 7th or 8th century CE, when Jewish traders first roamed the silk trading routes. Some historians even believe that Jews first came to China by way of ancient Persia following the destruction of Jerusalem by the Romans in 70 CE.

The most reliable evidence of the ancient Jewish presence in China comes from the city of Kaifeng, in what is now Henan province, where a synagogue is believed to have been built in 1163 CE and a Jewish community flourished. Although the synagogue was destroyed by fire, a number of stone slabs with inscriptions have been found as evidence of its existence. One slab deals with the passing down of the Jewish religion from Abraham to the prophet Ezra, whilst another details a number of familiar Jewish religious practices.

This Kaifeng community is believed to have numbered some 5,000 people. Their Chinese neighbours were apparently tolerant of them, despite their practice of circumcising males and their strange dietary laws that prohibited the eating of pork. Due to the isolation of this community from the mainstream of Jewish life, combined with assimilation and inter-marriage, the community eventually melded into the wider Chinese population. So much so, that the Jews eventually became indistinguishable from the other Chinese around them. After the last rabbi of Kaifeng died in the early part of the 19th century, the community was unable to sustain itself and gradually disappeared.

The Russian Jewish community was relatively new to the Shanghai scene, compared with the Sephardi Jewish community. The first Russian Jewish settler in Shanghai to become a permanent resident arrived in 1887.

The Russo-Japanese War of 1904-1905 sparked further arrivals of Russian Jews. They were Jews conscripted into the Russian army who endured a brutal anti-Semitic existence. After the humiliating defeat of the Russian forces at the hands of the Japanese, a number of these Russian Jewish soldiers decided not to return home, instead opting to try their luck in Shanghai. By 1907, the first Ashkenazi Russian synagogue was formally inaugurated, paving the way for the establishment of a community.

The next wave came about as a result of the First World War. Once again, Jewish soldiers were conscripted into the Russian army and their fate was no better than those who had fought for Russia ten years earlier. With the disintegration of the tsarist army in the wake of the revolution of 1917 and the atrocities during the ensuing civil war, more Russian Jewish veterans sought safety and a better life in Shanghai.

By 1924, there were 800 Russian Jews in Shanghai and they initially settled in Wayside, an area in the Hongkew district of the International Settlement. Later, as they prospered, they moved to the French Concession, which was a much more attractive residential area.

Then there were the Jews from Harbin. At its peak, Harbin was an important centre of Jewish life in China, particularly in intellectual and religious pursuits. Russian Jews had gravitated to it in the late 19th century, taking advantage of the benign economic and religious environment. A good proportion of them established businesses and, for a while, lived a comfortable existence. But this proved to be short lived as turmoil engulfed the settled Jewish community. In 1928, the Soviet government turned over the Chinese Eastern Railway to Chinese ownership and this brought to an end the protected status of many of the foreign-owned enterprises. Many members of Harbin's Jewish community decided to quit this precarious situation and seek a new life in Shanghai.

The next influx of Russian Jews from Harbin to Shanghai was propelled by the Japanese invasion of Manchuria in 1931. To 'legitimise' their control over this huge part of northern China, the Japanese kidnapped the last Manchurian emperor and installed him as a figurehead ruler over Manchuria, which they renamed Manchuko. Unfortunately for the Jews of Harbin, the Japanese rulers came under the spell of the large number of rabidly anti-Semitic White Russians living there and the result was mayhem for the remaining Jews and their institutions. The vulnerable fled to the safety of Shanghai.

By 1937, the Russian Jewish community in Shanghai had swelled to 4,000; a critical mass sufficient for an impressive network of communal institutions to be established. In that year, the Russian Jewish community, which had previously been considered part and parcel of the wider white Russian community, was recognised by the Shanghai Municipal Council as a separate communal association.

Next came the Jews from Vladivostok. Many of them were business people or 'capitalists', as the communists called them. As the communist system consolidated itself in the far eastern provinces of the former Russian empire, these Jews felt that they had no future under this new regime. They left their businesses behind and began to look for somewhere else to stake their future. My grandparents and my father were amongst those who settled upon Shanghai.

As residents of Shanghai, the majority of Russian Jews were 'stateless' in that they were not nationals of any country. They possessed no passports and unlike most of the other Europeans, had no official representatives to turn to in times of need.

The communal development of the Russian Jews of Shanghai was greatly enhanced by the arrival, from Vladivostok, of Rabbi Meir Ashkenazi, to become its Chief Rabbi. Meir Ashkenazi was born in Russia and arrived in Vladivostok after having completed his rabbinical studies. He became a Lubavitcher Hassid, a member of a very pious sect, which strictly observed the Jewish laws and traditions. He became engaged to the daughter of a venerable Jewish religious teacher, Rabbi Soloveichik and he married her in Harbin. He then moved to Shanghai in 1926, when the communists, who were atheists, started to make life difficult for him as a religious leader. My grandparents knew Rabbi Ashkenazi in Vladivostok and their friendship continued in Shanghai. I recall my grandparents talking about him in the warmest way.   He enjoyed the high regard of his own community as well as the Sephardi Jewish community. His crowning achievement was the erection of The New Synagogue in Rue Tenant de la Tour, in the French Concession in April 1941, where, by then, most of the Russian Jews lived.

The community soon established many institutions including a school, a hospital, a Talmud Torah for religious study, an old-age home called a 'shelter house', a mikveh (the ritual bath house for women), a burial association known as the Chevra Kadisha and, to complete the life-cycle circle, a cemetery.

As Shlema Moshinsky became financially successful he naturally gravitated towards a personal involvement in the affairs of the Russian Jewish community in Shanghai. He was a substantial contributor to the building of Rabbi Ashkenazi's new synagogue and, in recognition of this, his reserved seat was in the most honoured area of the synagogue. I remember sitting next to him or in the main part of the synagogue next to Father and looking up at Grandmother and Eva sitting upstairs with the other women. Grandfather was also involved with the Chevra Kadisha. Many years later, this would result in a great fuss being made over him at his funeral.

Grandfather also supported the world-wide effort to purchase land in Palestine to facilitate the establishment of Jewish settlers. In 1936 he acquired a choice piece of land in Haifa. Eventually, the land was taken over by the council for public purposes.

Like many prosperous manufacturers, Grandfather's attention eventually turned to real estate, firstly to provide a better place for us to live, and then, for investment income. He acquired land in a lane off Rue Doumer, the main thoroughfare of the well-to-do French Concession. In the late 1930s he commenced the planning of what was to become the Doumer Apartments, soon commissioning an architect called Gava Rabinovitch and a builder called Kooklin. Next to the Doumer Apartments was a two-story villa, which was also acquired for possible renovation later on.

For investment purposes, he also acquired two properties in Hongkew, an area north of Shanghai. It was then a poor and problematic district that eventually became the centre of fighting between the Japanese and the Chinese. Grandfather thought that these two properties held some promise, but he did not live long enough to see this promise realised.

To mark special occasions in our lives, various presents, made of silver, were commissioned to be hand made. A local jeweller, Mr Zourahoff, was kept busy by our family, creating beautiful decorative pieces including a silver menorah, an intricate cover for a writing pad, eggcups, spoons and a silver glass-holder for drinking tea, all of which I still possess.

Food was plentiful and I continued to be force fed, to ensure I looked rosy cheeked and full of good health. I played with the Chinese children in the locality of the factory and I went to the French Park with my amah or Eva to meet and play with the children of the other Russian Jewish families. On the weekends Father and Eva would take me to the cinemas and to more outings in the park. I recall these days with warmth. It was a very cocooned existence, our family apparently unaffected by the looming war which would so dramatically impact the lives of so many.

The silver Menorah that Mr Zourahoff created for the Moshinsky family

Ecole Municipale, 1941

6

STARTING SCHOOL

'A person's "face" is their most important personal possession.'
Miriam Moshinsky

In September 1939, two months after I turned five, my pleasant life took a new turn. I was enrolled to start at the Ecole Municipale, or the French school, as it was known, which was situated at the northern end of the French Park. The locality was familiar to me, and I was well prepared for this new stage.

We were still living above the factory in Rue Lafayette and my new school was only a few minutes' walk away. My amah walked me to school each morning and, in the early afternoon at the end of classes, she would be waiting to take me home. We used to walk through the French Park, playing with friends along the way. I have no idea what my amah did all day while I was in school.

There were approximately 300 children at the French school, from infants through to the Baccalaureate class, the entrance level for French universities. Most of the students were French, but there were also a significant number of Russian children, both Jewish and non-Jewish, as well as a sprinkling of Asian children from French Indo-China. The ethos and culture were decidedly French. All lessons were taught in French and French holidays were celebrated. On Bastille Day, a military parade of the French army and police was held in the French Park and we all attended.

I particularly remember the annual Christmas party. We were all assembled in the large school hall, dominated by a huge Christmas tree, and presents were handed out to every child in the lower grades, even the Jewish ones. This was a welcome gesture from the school, as a number of the students came from very poor families.

I started to make friends at school with a few of the Russian Jewish children, whose parents my grandparents and Father knew. I also became multilingual, speaking French at school, Russian at home and Chinese with my amah.

The year 1939 unfortunately ended on a tragic note. Late in December of that year Eva gave birth to a son, Boris, named after her brother who had died in Russia. Within a few days of birth, however, Boris developed some complications, from which he did not recover. I was in the factory when Father brought a very distraught Eva home. For some months there was immense sadness, which pervaded the atmosphere in the factory. Even the workers, with whom we were all quite close, shared our grief. It took the birth of Nathan, two years later, to lift the veil of sadness.

At that time, the increasingly ugly and bloody fighting between the Japanese and Chinese did not directly affect the European residents in Shanghai. But, paradoxically, the Second World War in distant Europe did impact upon my life. And so, because I was Jewish, in May 1941, after only two years, I had to leave the French school.

The Second World War was sparked off when Nazi Germany attacked Poland on the 1st September 1939. Following the spurning, by Nazi Germany, of the ultimatum issued by Britain and France to cease hostilities in Poland, these two countries declared war on Germany on the 3rd September 1939, and the Second World War officially commenced in Europe. After a short and brutal campaign, the German army overwhelmed the inferior Polish army and the Nazis occupied Poland until its liberation by the Soviet army in 1944. This was a tragedy for the Polish people, whose land was by then jointly occupied by the Nazi and Soviet armies. But it was especially tragic for the three million Jewish people of Poland. The Nazis annihilated nearly all of this thousand-year-old Jewish community.

Initially, in Western Europe, an eerie quietness was experienced. But, on the 9th April 1940, Nazi Germany, having digested its conquest of Poland, turned west with the invasion of Denmark and Norway, two defenceless countries. This was followed by the subjugation of Belgium and Holland, a prelude to the invasion of France, Germany's traditional enemy, in June 1940. Again, the German army won an easy victory, culminating in the capture of Paris on the 14th June 1940. The German army won easily, for two main reasons: first of all, the brilliant German army outflanked and then surrounded the sluggish and poorly led French army; secondly, and more importantly, France itself was a politically divided country. A significant proportion of the population was rabidly anti-Semitic and right wing, and they actually came to terms with the German occupation. So much so, that in July 1940, following the invasion and defeat of France, the Nazis permitted a pro-German semi-autonomous French government to be established. This Vichy French government, as it became known, based in the spa resort town of Vichy in southern France, shared the racist anti-Semitic ideology of its Nazi masters. Tragically, as a result, a large proportion of the French Jewish population eventually perished in the Holocaust.

Although Charles de Gaulle, a patriotic and charismatic general, established a French government-in-exile in London to prosecute the war against the Nazi occupiers, the Vichy government saw itself as the legitimate continuation of the pre-war French government. France, in 1939, was also a colonial power. While it wasn't as extensive as the British empire was then, it nevertheless had significant overseas colonies in North Africa, the Middle East and the Pacific Ocean. Amongst these colonial possessions, although not an actual colony, was the French Concession in Shanghai. These overseas 'possessions' fell under the influence of the Vichy government and so the French municipal authorities in Shanghai, led by the French Consul General, started leaning towards the anti-Semitic policies of its masters.

That is how the far-off conflict in Europe personally affected me, as a five year old in Shanghai. The anti-Semitic policies of the Vichy government trickled down to the authorities of the Shanghai French Concession and even to its school. As a Jew at the Ecole Municipale, it was anticipated at home that there would be a request for me to leave the school by the end of the school year in June 1941.

Apparently, it had been decided that I would attend an exclusive boarding school in Japan, from the beginning of September 1941. There was a lot of fuss about the school and much joy and satisfaction that I had been accepted. The school stipulated, in great detail, the uniform and other clothes that I should bring along with me. The school uniform consisted of short pants, long trousers, a blazer jacket, socks, shoes, cap and school tie, but I also had to take a whole bevy of other custom-made coats and shirts. The list even specified a beautiful large brown comb, which I cherished for many years afterwards. All these items were packed into a special new trunk, ready to travel to Japan with me.

However, after their usual summer trip to Beppu during the July-August holiday period of 1941, my grandparents felt apprehensive about this decision. Although it was still three months before the beginning of the open hostilities that culminated in the surprise bombing of Pearl Harbour on the 7th December 1941, the drums of war were already evident in Japan. By then, militarism was rampant there. My grandparents, through experience, were extremely perceptive people and they sensed that something ominous was in the air. Their suspicions were sufficiently strong that my enrolment was cancelled and I never went to the school in Japan. The risk of my being stranded there, as a result of the outbreak of war, was deemed to be too great.

And so I was 'grounded' in Shanghai, with a suitcase of the most wonderful set of clothes for which a child could wish. I can't recall what was done with the specially tailored school uniform, but the rest of the clothes were carefully rationed out over the war years until I grew out of them.

With the abandonment of the plan to send me to the elite international school in militaristic Japan, and my 'departure' from the Ecole Municipale because of Vichy France's anti-Semitism, the increasingly gloomy effects of war were beginning to impinge on my education. It was then decided to enrol me into a British school - Public Thomas and Hanbury, or PTH as it was known. PTH was modelled on an elite English 'public school'. And so, in September 1941, just after I turned seven, in yet another smart new uniform, I started at my second school in as many years.

My family appeared to have no qualms about sending me to a British school. They must have believed that the foreign concessions were inviolate. It is not hard to see why. The mighty Royal Navy had warships anchored in the Whangpoo River to ensure the protection of the British and other Europeans. Economically, Shanghai was booming. Its factories were flat out producing goods for shipment throughout the world, as the war in Europe was creating immense demands for a variety of merchandise. Who would want to upset this bountiful applecart?

And yet the reality was plainly there for all to see. The Japanese were ensconced in Hongkew, on the other side of Garden Bridge, their brutal sentries an ever-present reminder of their power over the Chinese populace. Their attitude to the British on the Shanghai Municipal Council was increasingly belligerent, and their military presence was growing and menacing.

Some of Shanghai's foreign residents felt a sense of foreboding as they read the *North China Daily News*, and other uncensored newspapers, about the growing confrontation between Japan and the United States. But many preferred not to think of it at all. They chose instead to lose themselves in the many culinary and sensuous delights in which Shanghai excelled.

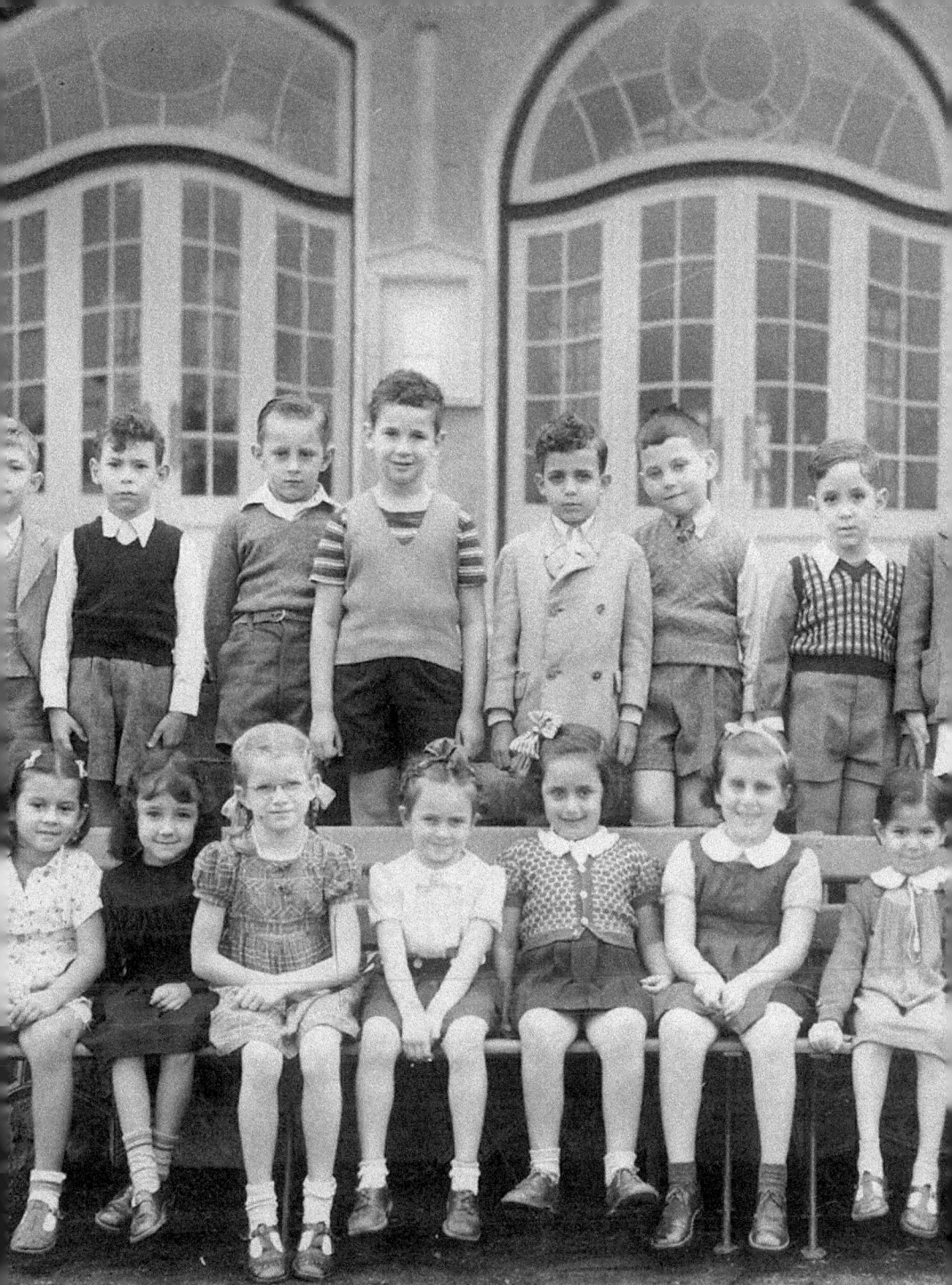

Ecole Municipale, 1940. Top left

Pearl Harbour, Hawaii on the
7th December 1941 after the
Japanese attack.

7

THE WAR IN THE PACIFIC BEGINS

'Yesterday, December 7, 1941 – a date that will live in infamy – the United States of America was suddenly and deliberately attacked by naval and airforces of the empire of Japan.'
President Franklin Delano Roosevelt in his address to both houses of Congress

On Sunday morning, the 7th December 1941, the unthinkable happened. In a totally unanticipated attack, 257 Japanese warplanes, taking off from an undetected fleet of aircraft carriers, bombed the great US naval base of Pearl Harbour in Hawaii. Heavy damage was inflicted on the United States Pacific Fleet. Simultaneously, in well-prepared and highly coordinated moves, the Japanese military struck at the Philippines, then a US possession, the British possessions in Malaya, and the Dutch East Indies, now known as Indonesia. Even relatively small Shanghai was directly affected. The Japanese military just moved across Garden Bridge and took over the largely British-run International Settlement.

It was quick, bloodless and extremely effective. No foreign forces could match the well-armed and highly motivated Japanese army and naval forces. In one stroke, nearly 75 years of European domination in a part of mainland China came to an end. The same fate awaited the British colony of Hong Kong and the other lesser 'concessions' in other coastal cities. Where we lived, however, the situation was different. The French Concession was technically under the control of Vichy France, ostensibly part of the 'Axis' group, the military alliance of Nazi Germany, Fascist Italy and Imperial Japan. Its status was therefore different to the International Settlement, considered to be British dominated. Technically, it was not invaded, but it still came under overt Japanese control, as Japanese troops freely moved around the concession.

By the following Monday morning, a whole new era dawned for a large number of 'Shanghailanders', depending on their national status. Citizens of Axis powers - Germans, Italians and Austrians - were unaffected. Citizens of states now at war with Japan, as a result of the Pearl Harbour attack, were the most vulnerable. In that category fell the British, the Americans and the Dutch, together with citizens of all the other nations aligned with the Allies. Their major institutions were either taken over or closed down. In addition, they were forced to abandon their homes and to undergo internment in camps set up by the Japanese outside of Shanghai.

By then, my grandparents and I were settled in the Doumer Apartments, which we had moved into in the previous year, and which was to be my home for the next eleven years. In the flat just below ours, lived an English family called the Bowns. Mr Bown was a middle level British civil servant, and his wife was a Russian. They had two children, a son Norman, who was a close friend, and an older sister called Evelyn. One cold morning, early in February 1942, I watched the four of them climbing aboard a truck carrying suitcases. I was extremely distressed and crying as I said goodbye to Norman. And that was the last we saw of them until August 1945, when they suddenly returned.

When the Bowns came back, we had them over for dinner and they recounted their experiences. They all looked reasonably healthy, but thinner. Mr Bown chain-smoked the American cigarettes that had become easily available. He said that the absence of cigarettes was probably the most difficult thing he had been forced to endure. Food had been in very limited supply and was strictly rationed, but he said that their Japanese guards fared no better regarding food. There appeared to be little or no physical maltreatment and there seemed to be an absence of hatred against the Japanese.

The Bown episode was the only personal experience I had of the effect of the war on the British and Americans of Shanghai. But I am sure that my grandparents and parents knew many others who endured the Japanese camps.

Although the Japanese attack on Pearl Harbour fully ushered in the Second World War in the Far East, there were still a number of neutral countries: Switzerland most notably; many South American countries; and interestingly enough, Portugal, even though it possessed the colony of Macau near Hong Kong. The citizens of these neutral countries could move about freely and carry on with their affairs, as best as circumstances permitted.

Soviet citizens were in a special category, and were also basically unaffected by the Japanese occupation. The Soviet Union became a major combatant from the 21st June 1941, when Nazi Germany also suddenly invaded her. However, with regard to Japan, she remained a non-combatant, or a 'neutral' power. Initially, Japan, as an active ally of Nazi Germany, considered throwing in its lot with its German allies and invading the Soviet Union. But with the war against China absorbing much of its military resources, and the alluring prizes of oil, rubber and other natural resources available in the Pacific region, the Japanese leadership decided against the attack. This 'non-combatant' arrangement turned out to suit both Japan and the Soviet Union. They treated each other as neutrals, a quite bizarre situation given their military involvements in other parts of the world.

This situation also affected the non-Soviet Russians in China and in Shanghai in particular. They had fled from the Soviet Union as a result of the 1917 Bolshevik revolution. But they were of different religious and cultural backgrounds. The most numerous were those of the old nobility, the sub-nobility and all those closely associated with the now deposed tsarist regime. They were Russian Orthodox by religion and very anti-communist in their politics. They were called 'White Russians', as opposed to the communist 'Reds', whose symbol was the red flag of the new communist state. Of course, having fled the revolution, they were not about to become citizens of this new Soviet state. A significant proportion of these White Russians were also anti-Semitic, which they had absorbed from their Russian Orthodox religion and the very anti-Jewish ethos of the now deposed tsarist regime, with which they strongly identified.

Overall, the White Russians fared poorly in the prosperous Shanghai of the 1920s and 1930s. With some exceptions, they were a dispirited group, finding it hard to come to terms with their new status as a non-privileged class. They knew little or no English and they became stuck in the lower rungs of the economic ladder, many just a cut above the Chinese. It must have been extremely humiliating for them to serve as storemen, drivers and entertainers in nightclubs and bars. For some of their women it was particularly galling to have to resort to menial work and even prostitution.

The lucky ones were seamstresses and housekeepers to the better-off families of Shanghai, catering to the needs of the wealthy, many of whom they looked down upon. In our household, my grandparents employed such a White Russian woman. Tonia was single and, as I recall, quite a simple woman. Tonia supervised the household, sometimes doing the cooking and performing most of the cleaning tasks.

This degradation of their status fed an extreme resentment against society, and again, some took it out on the Jews. Our synagogue was situated close to an area where many of the poor White Russians lived. And, on the major Jewish holidays when the synagogue was full, they would hurl stones at it. The brave ones among them came close enough to shout out anti-Semitic epithets.

Naturally, this unflattering picture of the White Russian community is a broad generalisation. There was also a middle class that was quite different. The Vinogradovs were a non-Jewish Russian family that became the first tenants of the Doumer Apartments. I became life-long friends with their son Alex, or Sasha as he was called. Mr Vinogradov was an engineer and worked for the Shanghai Power Company. Mrs Vinogradov stayed home to look after Alex and his younger brother Peter. Their coterie of friends was similar to them, middle class, and largely employed as professionals. Some of them took up Soviet citizenship when it was offered, and when economic conditions became very bad during the war, some even considered 'returning to the homeland'.

The Jewish refugees from Russia were poles apart from the White Russians. They generally 'hit the ground running' when they arrived in Shanghai. To be uprooted and to seek safety and opportunity in another locality was part of the age-old Jewish experience. They therefore suffered few of the traumas that the non-Jewish Russians experienced. The Russian Jewish refugees readily grasped the opportunity that this unbelievable laissez-faire economic environment provided and generally flourished in its wake. They brought with them their forward-looking outlook, an intellectual and religious culture, together with a strong sense of community. Soon the Russian Jews started to enjoy the prosperity that Shanghai's booming economy made possible.

The Russian Jews, like their non-Jewish counterparts, were, in the main, stateless. A small number did take up Soviet citizenship when it was offered. For the Japanese authorities, they were all part of the group to be left alone, as they were anxious not to antagonise the Soviets. The Japanese had enough on their plate prosecuting the Pacific War against the Americans.

At the bottom of the pile were the unfortunate Chinese, whose lives became even more miserable, with the exception of the few who decided to collaborate with the Japanese.

The Russian Jews found themselves in a unique situation. Probably for the first time in their unhappy history, they were in a preferred position with respect to the other Jews. The Japanese interred the Sephardi Jews, who carried British papers, and the 'refugee' Jews from Germany, Austria and Poland were soon forced to relocate into a specially designated area in Hongkew.

The Russian Jews intensified their efforts by developing their communal institutions and, where possible, establishing organisations to assist the less fortunate.

Mr and Mrs Vinogradov in their lounge, Doumer Apartments

Betar, 1942. Bottom right

8

THE SHANGHAI JEWISH
SCHOOL AND BETAR

'I devote my life to the rebirth of the Jewish state,
with a Jewish majority, on both sides of the Jordan.'
Ze'ev Jabotinsky, introducing the Betar oath in 1934

The Japanese takeover of the International Settlement meant yet another change of school for me. The Japanese closed down Public Thomas and Hanbury and my parents were forced to search for another school. I do not know how many Russian Jewish students were affected by the school's closure, but probably not many. A significant portion of the student population were children of British and American nationals, who had already been forced to accompany their parents to the internment camps set up outside Shanghai by the Japanese.

A decision was made to enrol me into the Shanghai Jewish School (SJS), in Seymour Road, not far from home. SJS was a good example of the dedication and generosity of one of the most remarkable Jewish communities in the history of the Diaspora. The school's origins go back to 1931, when Mr Perry, a wealthy Sephardi Jewish resident, left a substantial bequest to be applied to the establishment of a school for Sephardi children. A fellow Sephardi Jewish millionaire, Elly Kadoorie, matched Perry's bequest of 50,000 silver taels, and a modern school, with well-lit large classrooms and other spacious facilities was constructed. Initially it was intended to provide a good and inexpensive, general and Jewish education for the poorer Sephardi families. In time, it lived up to the full meaning of its name and admitted the children of the growing Russian Jewish community. When the initial trickle of Central European Jewish refugees turned into a flood in the late 1930s, the school admitted them too.

I was happy at this school, and I made a number of lasting friendships there. It was my first school with a Jewish student body. More importantly, it was there that I first came into contact with non-Russian Jews. They were the Sephardi and Central European Jews.

When I entered the school in September 1942, there were still a number of Sephardi Jews, but they were dwindling in number. Unlike the Russian and Central European Jews, who fled oppressive regimes and were mainly 'stateless' with no formal nationalities or passports, the Sephardi Jews were generally British subjects, originally from British-controlled countries such as Iraq and India.

The Sephardi Jews of Shanghai originated in Baghdad, the capital of Iraq and the home of one of the oldest Jewish communities in the world. Like many of their religious compatriots, they were shrewd and successful traders, tapping into the growing trading possibilities of an emergent British empire, extending from London to India. This took them to India in the first part of the 19th century, many of them settling in Bombay, now Mumbai, India's largest trading centre. They worked closely with the British in the growing cotton and opium trades, and in parallel with them, extended their trading networks to the British empire in the East, first Singapore, then Hong Kong and eventually Shanghai, as it assumed its trading and commercial importance.

What made the Sephardi Jewish community of Shanghai so unique was the presence of a number of brilliant and ambitious entrepreneurial families. Their names - Sassoon, Kadourie, Hardoon, Ezra, and Abrahams - became by-words for flair and success, and they were often called the 'Rothschilds of the East'. Importantly, from a Jewish perspective, their wealth did not in any way diminish their commitment to their faith. They were fully committed to their communal responsibilities, both in assisting the poorer families in their own community, as well as the many other Jews who increasingly sought refuge in Shanghai.

The first Sephardi family to succeed financially was the Sassoon family, who were already extremely rich from their trading activities in Bombay, before establishing a branch in Shanghai in 1845. Part of this family's success was due to the talented Sephardis they employed in their enterprises, many of whom then left to form their own successful businesses. They were ambitious people and did not rest on the laurels of their fortunes made in the opium, tea, silk, wool and cotton trades. They expanded into land holdings and eventually became some of the largest landlords of Shanghai. They also extended themselves in businesses such as banks, insurance, public transport and breweries. Their lifestyles were legendary; they built the most splendid mansions, threw extravagant parties and fully participated in the beautiful life of Shanghai.

A number of the successful Sephardi community members immersed themselves in the public life of the city, serving as councillors on the all-important Shanghai Municipal Council (SMC). One, Silas Hardoon, served on both the English-dominated SMC, as well as the Counseille Municipale Francais, the controlling body of the French Concession.

From a communal point of view, the Sephardi Jews, very early in their Shanghai presence, established synagogues as well as a cemetery, called the Shehita Cemetery. Due to differences in religious and cultural traditions, the two communities, the Sephardi and the Ashkenazi Russians, largely kept to themselves.

It was left to my generation to blend the differences and to seek a greater sense of community within the Shanghai Jewish School. I had a number of friends from the Sephardi community, both rich and poor, and we visited each other's homes. What the wealthiest ones thought of our comfortable apartment in the Doumer Apartments, I do not know. But I do recall being invited to visit the mansion of one of my Sephardi friends. I was struck by the size of the home and the magnificence of the surrounding grounds, the manicured lawns and the English-style gardens. Vivid in my memory was the library, a room of immense proportions, fully lined with books and comfortable Chesterfield armchairs.

In dealing with the flood of Jewish refugees pouring in from Nazi Europe, the two communities really came together. The Sephardi Jews, by far the wealthier of the two communities, rose to the challenge and were at the forefront of refugee aid.

Within the grounds of the school was a beautiful Sephardi synagogue, Ohel Rachel. During the war, this synagogue was largely unused. Between the synagogue and the actual school building was a soccer ground, soccer being the dominant sport. At times we would play soccer against the 'Hongkew' boys, the Central European Jews who were confined by the Japanese in that section of Shanghai.

Looking back, the education at the Shanghai Jewish School was good, and my time there was stress free. The principal of the school was Mr Kahans, whose son, Daniel, was a good friend of mine. In keeping with the schooling of those years, certain basic skills were specifically taught and insisted upon. It was years before computers existed. And even typewriters, although quite prevalent, were used only for business correspondence. All inter-personal correspondence was written by hand and therefore its legibility was important. Fortunately neat handwriting came naturally to me, and I recall receiving silver and sometimes even gold stars on my assignments to testify to the quality of my handwriting.

During the war years, I also became a member of Betar, a Zionist youth movement that was part of the right-wing 'Herut' movement founded by Vladimir Jabotinsky, a native of Odessa. The Betar youth movement, and its adult parent, the Herut, was the dominant Zionist movement in the Far East. Zionism occupied a prominent place in the aspirations of Russian Jews, a reflection of their long-standing sense of helplessness and lack of acceptance in the societies in which they lived. Although the Sephardi Jews were not as ardent supporters of Zionism, it was one of them, Nissim Ezra, who helped found the Shanghai Jewish School and who actually pioneered Zionism in China. He established and financed the first newspaper devoted to this cause, *Israel's Messenger.* Ezra went on to introduce the concept of a Jewish homeland to Dr Sun Yat-sen, the revered father of modern China, who is on record as a supporter of Zionism.

In Shanghai, Betar's early activities were devoted to education and physical development. Later, military training was successfully introduced and the Shanghai Volunteer Corps, the militia of the European residents, was persuaded to include a Jewish unit within its ranks.

The Betar group initially met within the walls of the Jewish Club, then in Bubbling Well Road, in the International Settlement. As it developed in popularity, the congestion in the club was relieved by a generous supporter donating a top floor apartment of his father's house on Avenue

Joffre as the new clubhouse. There, in my uniform consisting of a brown shirt, a neckband and a military cap, I first encountered the map of Palestine, the future home of the Jewish people, and I learnt patriotic songs and the stories of Zionist heroes. The spirit of the group was very inclusive; I enjoyed going there and I formed life-long friendships with Reuben Wekselman, Joe Toochinsky, George Tomchinsky and Ika Joffe among others.

After the war, the Jewish Club moved to new and spacious premises in Rue Pichon, which contained a number of buildings within the extensive grounds. One of these was set aside for use by Betar, a very generous gesture reflective of the support it enjoyed from the leaders of the Russian Jewish community. The club included an auditorium for the staging of plays, meeting rooms and sports grounds where we performed low-level military training, such as crawling along the ground and pretending to throw hand-grenades.

The Shanghai Jewish School, 1943. Middle row, second from the right

Section of the Ward Road Heim in Hongkew, 1940

9

A HAVEN FOR JEWISH REFUGEES

*'In those days the world was divided into two kinds
of countries: countries that want to be rid of Jews
and those that refuse to accept them.'*
Chaim Weizmann to the Evian Conference on
Refugees in 1938

The German and Austrian Jewish students at the Shanghai Jewish School were children from the large influx of refugees of the late 1930s. The boys and girls were fair skinned, unlike the darker Sephardi kids; they spoke English poorly, but were good at sport, particularly football.

Their parents were trying to find their feet in Shanghai. Some of them were well-educated middle-class Jews who had only recently experienced the shock of travelling from their 'civilised' communities in Central Europe, to this bizarre city in the East. Some had financial means, whilst many were assisted. Eventually a number of them started to establish themselves in the laissez-faire economy of Shanghai.

Shanghai had provided an improbable haven for these desperate Jews. Not long before they arrived in numbers which would eventually dwarf the size of the existing Sephardi and Russian Jewish communities, few would have believed that these Jews would be subject to this particular ordeal. The Jews of Germany numbered approximately 500,000, whilst there were 185,000 Jews in Austria in the early 1930s, when the bell started to toll for them. Until that time, arguably, nowhere in the world were Jews in such a fortunate position. German and Austrian Jews participated in the emancipation of Western and Central European Jewry from the age-old shackles of Christendom, in the post-Napoleonic era, with great zeal. The Jews of these two countries immersed themselves wholeheartedly in their respective societies and, in the process, discarded many of the vestiges of their past separateness. Their readiness to assimilate was accompanied with considerable success and distinction in the arts, sciences, literature, business and the professions. In the realm of religious practice, a new and seemingly more progressive tone was developed and embraced.

For a while this illusion of equality and acceptance was strongly believed in. But beneath this veil of equality lurked the demon of anti-Semitism, rooted in the German national psyche and nurtured through hundreds of years of hateful indoctrination. Many of these sentiments became manifest during the economic turmoil of the German economy in the aftermath of the Great Depression, which began in the United States in

1929. But these ominous signs were ignored and Hitler came to power in 1933, replete with his own psychotic hatred of the Jews. The Jewish communities were totally unprepared to deal with the situation.

The advent of a Nazi government in Germany became the platform for the launching of an organised terror campaign against the Jews: random, as well as calculated physical assaults; the confiscation of property; and the deprivation of basic civil rights through the promulgation of draconian racial laws. It was not even possible to escape the impact of this situation through converting out of Judaism. Even in the Christian conquest of Spain and Portugal, those Jews who were prepared to fully convert to Christianity were generally accepted as Christians and allowed to remain. But this new assault was not only firmly rooted in age-old religious intolerance, its dynamic was also racial. The racial laws promulgated in Nuremberg on 15th September 1935 defined, in obsessive detail, the level of diminution of 'Jewish blood', through generations-old inter-marriage, that was acceptable. For the majority of Jews of Germany, however, despite the fact that a considerable number had married non-Jewish Germans, escape was not possible. Even if one's own low level of Jewish life and practice made it tempting to shake off Judaism in order to escape this new scourge, one was entrapped by virtue of birth, not conviction.

We all now know of the tragedy of the Holocaust and the complete annihilation of European Jewry. But in the beginning, the situation was quite different; most German Jews simply could not grasp this new and dangerous reality. They were steeped in the belief that what they were painfully experiencing was no more than a passing storm. After all, they were living in arguably the most civilised society in the world. Many were rooted in successful businesses and professions that provided a comfortable lifestyle, which was, understandably, hard to give up. And where would they go? Many avenues were already closed to them, as the world economic depression and the resulting unemployment caused many countries to restrict drastically their immigration intakes. So, many decided to tough things out.

Later, I would empathise with their dilemma, for my own family's situation in 1949 was similar. By the time it was clear that Shanghai would fall to the communist forces, it was too late. We had to get out as quickly as possible and we also had the problem of where to go. For us, finding a destination became an extremely difficult issue, as it was for the remaining German and Austrian Jews. The irony was that their destination of last resort became Shanghai, while in my family's case, we were stranded in Shanghai and seeking to leave it.

The world was experiencing an economic depression and no nation was prepared to issue entry visas, which would add to its own severe unemployment problems. The Jews were under ceaseless pressure from the German Nazis to emigrate, while finding all the obvious avenues of resettlement closed to them. This was starkly evident at the Evian Conference, called by President Roosevelt, to try to find a solution for what was then the world's principal refugee problem. The conference took place in the French town, known for its bottled drinking water, during July 1938. Thirty-two nations participated, but few were willing to open their doors to Jewish immigrants. Australia was one of the more generous countries, but unfortunately, not all the entry visas could be availed upon as the outbreak of the war in the following year made travel virtually impossible.

With such an impasse, the thoughts of many turned to Shanghai, even though its distance and dubious reputation were deterrents to solid, middle-class Jews. Ironically, whilst the Nazi authorities were willing to promote Shanghai as a destination, some Jewish organisations were still doubtful of it as a suitable haven. The Germans initiated serious discussions with the Japanese and Chinese authorities for the admission of Jews. Plans were even drawn up to charter ships to enable the transport of large numbers of Jews. Eventually, in the late 1930's, as the world's doors remained closed and the pressures of Nazi attacks became unbearable, some 15,000-18,000 Jews made the long journey to this bizarre outpost of European settlement, where no visas were required.

Initially, these new arrivals found it very difficult. It was one thing to purchase a ticket on an ocean liner and arrive at its destination unhindered. It was another thing to support oneself when one got there. Many of the arrivals were professionals or middle-class shopkeepers and manufacturers. Most had been forced to leave the bulk of their assets behind. Despite Shanghai's prosperity, it was daunting for these traumatised arrivals, particularly as there was no state institution that saw their plight as a moral responsibility.

Amid all their difficulties, a silver lining started to appear. Their plight did not go unnoticed by the two Jewish communities present in Shanghai in the 1930s. Although these two communities generally had little to do with each other, they rallied to the cause of extending a helping hand to fellow Jews in distress. They formed a body to deal with the situation called the South Asia Central Refugee Association. The newcomers were accommodated and also provided with food and assistance for integrating into society. Although many found it difficult to make the transition into a new trade or profession, a number did begin to do well. It was hoped, that in time, more and more of them would successfully entrench themselves in Shanghai's economy. For a while this even seemed possible.

A relatively small group of ultra-orthodox Jewish refugees also started arriving in Shanghai in August 1941, while I was on holidays with my grandparents in Beppu, Japan. One of them later became my first private Hebrew tutor. Unlike the predominantly secular Central European Jews who had recently arrived in Shanghai, most of the group consisted of rabbis and students of various yeshivot, centres of advanced Talmudic learning, in Poland and Lithuania. Their extraordinary saga innocently began when they tried to escape the flow-on effect of coming under the atheistic rule of the Soviet regime, following the signing of the German-Soviet Non-Aggression Pact of August 1939.

Integrating these orthodox Jews into the fabric of Shanghai's secular and commercial culture was virtually impossible, whatever the numbers. They were not trained for normal work, their dietary needs required special attention and they had to engage in Talmudic study as a group. They required considerable support and were accommodated at the Sephardi Beth Aharon Synagogue and at the Russian Jewish Club. What they did provide Shanghai with was unique: an active centre of Jewish learning where the hundreds of scholars from the Mir Yeshivah and remnants of some other yeshivot could continue what their forebears had done for centuries before in Eastern Europe.

Even after December 1941, following the outbreak of the war in the Pacific and the Japanese takeover of the rest of Shanghai, all of these newcomers were basically left alone. Although the Japanese were allies of Nazi Germany, they did not automatically follow its anti-Semitic policies. In fact, in certain quarters there was a certain empathy with the Jewish people, based on a respect for strong family ties and resourcefulness in the face of adversity.

But on the 18th February 1943, well into the depths of the war, disaster struck. By proclamation, all refugees who arrived in Shanghai after 1937, in other words, the bulk of the refugees who had fled the Nazis, were confined to live in a small, designated area in Hongkew among the existing Chinese. Although the proclamation did not specifically mention the Jews, its effect was to incarcerate them. They were given just three months to uproot themselves. The area designated was in a very confined and poor area. It was a mindless hardship; even those living on the other side of road to the designated area had to make the move. Although no walls were actually constructed, as in the infamous Warsaw Ghetto, for all practical purposes it was a European-style ghetto bizarrely replicated on the Asian mainland. Some movement in and out of this area was permitted and the authority for this was vested in a psychotic and diminutive Japanese officer called Goya. He relished humiliating and inflicting physical violence on the Jews who had to queue to obtain their passes to leave the ghetto for other parts of the city.

It was assumed that this action by the Japanese was carried out at the urging of the Germans, as a notorious Nazi officer was based in the Far East. Other evidence cast doubt on this theory, so the whole exercise had a mysterious undertone to it. In any event, the vast majority of those who fled for their lives from Nazi Germany found themselves confined in Hongkew right up until the end of the war.

PROCLAMATION

Concerning restrictions of residence and business of stateless refugees:

I: Due to military necessity, places of residence and business of the stateless refugees in the Shanghai area shall hereafter be restricted to the undermentioned area in the International Settlement: east of the line connecting Chaufoong Road, Muirhead Road and Dent Road; west of Yangtzepoo Creek; north of a line connecting East Seward Road and Wayside Road; south of the boundary of the International settlement.

II: The stateless refugees at present resident and/ or carrying on business in the district other than the above area shall remove their place of residence and/or business into the area designated above by May 18, 1943.

III: Persons other than the stateless refugees shall not remove into the area mentioned in Article I without permission of the Japanese authorities.

IV: Persons who will have violated this proclamation or obstructed its enforcement shall be liable to severe punishment.

Commander-in-Chief of the Imperial Japanese Army
In the Shanghai Area.
Commander-in-Chief of the Imperial Japanese Navy
In the Shanghai Area
February 18, 1943

With Father outside th[e]
Doumer Apartments, 194[ ]

10

MORE ON LIFE IN SHANGHAI

*'Get a good education, so that you can
keep your wealth in your head.'*
Abe Moshinsky

By the beginning of 1942, the first year of war, as far as the foreign communities of Shanghai were concerned, I had already settled into the Doumer Apartments with my grandparents. Father and Eva continued to live in the apartment above the factory. Once or twice a week, I went over there for dinner and sometimes I would sleep overnight, if there was no school the next day. The relationship between Eva and myself was very good. From the start, she went out of her way to do as much as a natural mother would, often spoiling me and looking after me when I was ill. Over time, I developed a special bond and affection for her.

Eva was thrilled when, towards the end of the year, on the 12th November, Nathan was born, healthy and well. Father, Eva, Nathan and his amah, continued to occupy the apartment over the factory for another year.

The apartment I shared with my grandparents had a small entrance hall, with a kitchen leading off it. We had a large lounge-dining room with big windows and a balcony looking out onto the front garden. My grandparents' spacious bedroom also led to the balcony. My bedroom had two single beds in it, one for me, and one for Tonia, our Russian servant. Our bathroom had a toilet, a basin and a good size bath, but no shower.

Early in 1943, the apartment across the hallway from us became vacant and it was decided that Father, Eva and Nathan should move in. As a result, the family took over the whole first floor, which was an ideal arrangement.

We often ate together, usually in the evenings, when we were all at home. After Grandfather died, we alternated dining rooms; a banging on the common wall dividing the two dining rooms would indicate which apartment we would eat in that night.

The combined household staff consisted of four: Tonia and three Chinese servants. Tonia cleaned and supervised the household. Sometimes she cooked, when our cook had time off. We did not look forward to her cooking, for her culinary skills were average. She used to irritate us before serving her meals, loudly protesting that she had spoilt the dinner and that it was terrible. We would then politely say that it was fine, and continue to eat.

Our Chinese cook was tall, stocky and quite dignified in appearance. He spoke Russian and English. He arrived early each morning laden with fruit, vegetables, meat and other provisions from the market. He used to place the fruit and vegetables in a bathtub filled with water and some potassium permanganate was poured in to act as disinfectant. Apparently the fertiliser used by the Chinese market gardeners was human manure. Each morning, he also filled a dozen bottles with boiled water, left them to cool and then put them into the refrigerator. This was our drinking water supply, as water drunk straight from the tap would certainly cause sickness. Then, each morning, the 'wash amah' would turn up. She scrubbed everybody's dirty washing by hand in the bathtub and hung it outside to dry. She was also in charge of the ironing. Finally, there was my amah, who was, by then, assigned to Nathan as I had become too old to have one. This was our permanent household right up until 1952, when the family left Shanghai.

Most socialising took place in Shanghai's many restaurants and at the Jewish Club. But Jewish holidays, including Passover Seders, Rosh Hashanah feasts and the breaking of the fast on Yom Kippur, were always enjoyed at home. Friday nights were festive occasions at the Jewish Club, so Erev Shabbat dinners at home were not a regular event.

Grandfather, although not very observant, was quite traditional. He would sometimes go to the Russian Jewish synagogue on Saturday mornings. On the High Holidays we would all go. I would either sit with Father in the front or go to sit with Grandfather at his special seat near Rabbi Ashkenazi. Grandfather used to introduce me proudly to the other important members of the congregation.

There was always a lot of talking going on during the religious services. When Rabbi Ashkenazi was getting ready to deliver the sermon, all the children would file out. Although considered very erudite, the rabbi was not a dynamic speaker. Also, he delivered his sermons in Yiddish, which none of us understood. Outside, we used to play, gossip and sometimes flirt, in the very small front yard of the synagogue. During Pesach, we played games with walnuts in the front yard. We all knew each other and the atmosphere was fun and very friendly.

Before Yom Kippur, the synagogue served as the collection point for donations to the community's poor and needy. Each year, a few hours before the start of the Kol Nidrei service, I was sent with a wad of Chinese currency and instructions on how much to place on each of the plates earmarked for the various causes. One of the groups we financially supported in this way was the synagogue's male choir. It consisted mainly of German and Austrian Jews who were already living in Hongkew and who had to be bussed in to attend and sing at the services.

At home, sumptuous dinners with the usual Jewish trimmings - gefilte fish, chopped liver, herring, pickled cucumber and chicken soup - were dished up following the High Holiday services. The whole family would gather together at the extended dining-room table in our apartment. On Yom Kippur, Grandfather would do 'the Kapparot', whirling a live hen over his head several times, while reciting a prayer. The family always fasted on Yom Kippur and from the age of eleven, I started fasting 'practice runs'. The first year I fasted for a few hours, and the next year, for half a day. At Betar, we would boast to each other how long we had lasted without food or drink.

Every Pesach, we had a traditional Seder, with Grandfather leading the service. I used to recite the 'Manishtana', the age-old four questions. Grandfather hid an afikoman and I had to find it and then surrender it for a present, in order for the Seder service to be concluded. One year, I decided to exploit this practice. For some time I had wanted to get a bicycle to ride to school and around the streets. A number of my friends already had one and I envied them. But my grandparents were worried that I would have an accident or that I would be kidnapped, as Shanghai had experienced a number of kidnappings of children from wealthier families. All my pleadings were to no avail. So after one of the Seder dinners, I decided not to surrender the afikoman before extracting a promise that I would get a bicycle. That evening, I recall, was a long one. But I would not relent. Finally, Father came up with a compromise. I would get the bicycle, but he would get one also, and would accompany me as I rode to school. That is not what I had envisaged, but I agreed to the compromise. So, two bicycles were purchased and for a few days I rode to school with him following behind. Naturally, it was most embarrassing. Fortunately, after about a week, Father gave up on the idea of riding to school with me and reverted back to riding to the factory in his personal rickshaw.

My religious education was a matter of concern to my grandparents. Initially I was enrolled into a cheder, run by very orthodox rabbis. It was conducted out of a dingy and smelly room in a decrepit building off Avenue Joffre. I hated the place. The teaching was very old fashioned and consisted of learning prayers by rote, for hours at a time. If we slipped up in our Hebrew pronunciation, our knuckles were swiftly rapped with a ruler. After a few months of this, I announced my refusal to continue with the classes. So Grandmother hired a personal tutor. He was one of Shanghai's many refugee rabbis, from a noted yeshivah in Europe, who had escaped from Nazi persecution. Shanghai's wealthier Russian Jewish community members deemed it a social service to employ them, so, on several afternoons every week, while other children played in the laneway, I was stuck for an hour with this elderly person. Unfortunately, his system of teaching was not much better than at the cheder: still the same repeating of long passages from various Hebrew books, again and again, until I got it right. When I complained to Grandmother, she would say that one day I would appreciate having been taught by such an eminent person. She did not relent, and for years I had to endure these lessons.

The years of war did not affect our family's livelihood, despite the fact that the American Hazelwood Company was taken over by the Japanese. Ice cream continued to be consumed in summer, chocolate boxes were still in demand in winter, and the Shanghai Cardboard Box Factory continued to meet those demands. The Jewish Club remained fully operational, without any interference by the Japanese, and it continued to be the social hub for my family and a centre for Jewish celebrations, like the annual Purim fancy dress party, which Father and Eva regularly attended. The Betar youth group kept me busy after school and on Sundays.

Amid all this normality, there were instances to remind us, the privileged few, that there was a war going on. The Japanese had closed down the main English language newspaper, the authoritative *North China Daily News*, which had been in continuous publication since 1875. Listening to foreign broadcasts emanating from the Allied side was also forbidden. This may have affected the grown-ups, but not us. What did inconvenience us was the banning of American and British films. Our favourite Tarzan, Laurel and Hardy, Zorro and cowboy movies were no longer being screened.

All was not lost, however. The Soviet Union produced films and newsreels, radio programs and newspapers and these continued to be available, as it was not at war with Japan. Everyone relied on them to satisfy a voracious appetite for news of the war. It was all subject to control by the Soviet propaganda machine, but it was better than nothing. I can still picture Father trying to coax some response from our old art deco radio, as listening to the news was a ritual. We also had a very large map, on which Father used to plot, with coloured pins, the progress of battles on the European front. At the Soviet Club, every Sunday afternoon, there were newsreels shown of these battles. The Vinogradovs were members of the Soviet Club and I used to go there with them whenever Alex was taken along. These films did not really take the place of Tarzan, but going to the Soviet Club provided an opportunity to make new friends and to have some fun. Because the newsreels were quite boring to us, we used to play games, simulating the fighting between the Russians and the Germans.

Between school, Betar and the Soviet Club, life was quite busy, but pleasant. Nevertheless, as the war progressed and I grew older, I started to notice the suffering of the Chinese population, which was under the complete domination of the Japanese. Despite the fact that the Japanese claimed they were fighting the western powers on behalf of all Asians, they acted as cruel colonial conquerors. The plight of the Chinese was evident to all. From the humiliating searches and treatment meted out to those who needed to cross Garden Bridge, to the public beatings and the grinding poverty, their suffering was indeed great. There were beggars everywhere and the sight of so many horribly maimed was stomach churning. But the most pitiful were the mothers sitting on the sidewalks, with their young ones wailing from hunger. Most of them were homeless, eking out an existence by begging on the streets, day and night. The stench was overpowering. But it was even worse in winter. After a cold snap at night, many of the babies literally froze. And we could not escape all this, as often we had to step over the frozen babies on our way to school. We were all so warmly dressed and about to enter heated classrooms. I do not know what effect this had on the others; curiously, we rarely discussed this among ourselves. But I personally found it difficult to take. Whenever I had some loose change in my pocket, I would always drop it in the begging bowls. The sight of those frozen babies in the mornings will always be with me.

For the first part of the war, until the end of 1943, Shanghai was not subject to bombing. By then however, courtesy of *Tass*, the Soviet news service, there was a perception that the tide of war had turned in favour of the Western Allies. I recall whispers at home of 'the second front', as the expected Allied landings in Western Europe were termed. Nobody had any idea how Japan would be defeated. The Japanese military presence was omnipresent.

Although food was starting to be scarce, and rationing had begun, everything was somehow miraculously available to those who could afford the exorbitant black market prices. The Moshinskys must have been in that category, for I do not recall any want. In winter, when I would come home late from a Betar meeting, Grandmother would be there waiting with my favourite dish of hot boiled potatoes, sour cream and schmaltz herring. The Vinogradovs, on the other hand, were more indicative of how other Europeans, with limited resources, lived. Mr Vinogradov, working for the now Japanese controlled Shanghai Power Company, was on a fixed salary, so the increasing food prices were eroding their living standard. They had to be much more careful. When I visited Alex, I could feel Mrs Vinogradov's quandary between being hospitable to a guest and her concern that their fragile situation did not permit this. On one occasion, I recall her slicing some bread so thinly that I could almost see through it. And then, with horror, I saw her spreading lard over it, instead of the butter I was used to at home. Grandmother appreciated all this and encouraged me to invite Alex over to our place. For him, it was a real treat to eat the delicacies Grandmother provided.

As 1944 dawned, word reached Shanghai of the Nazi atrocities against the Jews of Europe. A protest meeting was called at the Jewish section of the cemetery, past Hongkew, which I attended with my family. The Japanese must have sanctioned the meeting, despite the fact that the protest was about their wartime ally, Nazi Germany. I recall that there were a lot of people there. It was cold and there were many speeches in Yiddish, as well as in Russian. The news was especially worrying to the German and Austrian Jews, segregated in the Hongkew ghetto, as many of them had left relatives back home.

On a happier note, word also reached Shanghai of the successful Allied landing in Normandy, the fabled 'second front'. There was much whispering about, what clearly seemed to be, the beginning of the end of the war against Nazi Germany.

Eva and Abe dressed up for the Jewish Club Purim party

Left: The Doumer Apartments
Above: With Eva and Nathan, 1943

Grandfather's tombstone at a
Jewish cemetery, Shanghai

11

GRANDFATHER'S DEATH

'What will happen to us now?'
Miriam Moshinsky

The year 1944 ended on a tragic note for the family, with the death of Grandfather, our patriarch. Shortly after the Jewish New Year and Yom Kippur, he was rushed to the Jewish hospital. I remember being taken to visit him there, in a private room. The visit was very sombre, with everybody sighing. His face had pallor to it and I suspect that he knew he was dying. As I learned later, by the end of 1944, specialised medication was not obtainable in Shanghai, even on the black market. Grandfather had an infection, possibly pneumonia, and penicillin could have cured him. But that was not to be. He died on the 7th December 1944 at the age of 60.

In keeping with Jewish tradition, a funeral was arranged for the next day. Given his prominence in the community, it would be a large funeral, as just about everybody in the Russian Jewish community wanted to pay their respects. There was, however, a problem. The day of the funeral was the anniversary of the Japanese bombing of Pearl Harbour. This was a very sensitive date as far as the Japanese were concerned, and there was a risk that the large procession from the synagogue, on Route Tenant de la Tour, to the cemetery in Hongkew would look like a demonstration. Thankfully, permission from the Japanese authorities was duly granted.

Grandfather's body was carried on what was called a catafalque, a carriage on wheels pushed by a number of men. It was a long and slow procession, on a cold day. We had to provide strong and warm walking boots for the men engaged in the pulling of the catafalque as their flimsy shoes were not up to the task. At the cemetery, another service was held, and my grandfather was then interred.

Following the funeral, there were seven days of prayer, with a 'minyan' of a minimum of ten adult Jewish men. Grandmother and Father sat 'shiva' for the entire seven days and Father did not shave. In keeping with Jewish religious tradition, all the mirrors in the house were covered with sheets and Father made a tear in his suit jacket to signify mourning. Grandmother was completely distraught, continuously wailing, 'What will happen to us now?' This was extremely hard on Father psychologically. For, in addition to losing a father, as an only son, he had to assume the mantle of running a substantial business during a very difficult time. He could have done with a more outward demonstration of confidence. Grandmother never seemed to have confidence in him. I suspect that it originally stemmed from her disapproval over his first marriage to my mother, as well as the fact that he was not, by nature, the same tough and resourceful businessman that his father had been.

The minyanim over the seven days are vividly etched in my memory as an exercise in social service, as well as religious practice. Early each morning, while it was still dark and cold, and again every evening, the participants would roll up. After the first two days, fewer friends came. The rest appeared to be poor and hungry and, I suspected, they came in search of warmth and food. Our apartment had central heating and I remember them huddling around the radiators. After prayers, the participants were generously fed the only decent food they would eat that day. Throughout all this, I never heard any words of complaint. It was something that was expected of us and we shared willingly and graciously.

After the seven days of mourning, life returned to normal, but with one exception. Father went every morning and every evening to the synagogue to say 'kaddish' for Grandfather, a practice expected of him and which he carried out diligently. I would often accompany him. We would walk to the synagogue and back home, to the Doumer Apartments, talking along the way. The exact subjects I cannot recall, but I fondly remember the bonding experience, as Father was a very kind and personable individual. After twelve months, the daily journey to the synagogue stopped, to be replaced by the annual 'yahrzeit' and we always went together.

Japanese Emperor Hirohito

12

THE FINAL YEAR OF WAR

*'The war situation has developed not necessarily to
Japan's advantage, while the general trends of the
world have all turned against her interest.'*
Emperor Hirohito, announcing Japan's surrender on
the 14th August 1945

In 1945 things started to become ominous. The Japanese military presence became more aggressive. There were more troops and more restrictions on movement. Over-flights by American warplanes, which began in June 1944, became more frequent, apparently targeting the harbour installations, although there was no bombing of Shanghai itself. The American planes were mainly the high-flying B-29s, which the Japanese anti-aircraft guns could not reach. The Japanese retaliated by commandeering nearly all of Shanghai's tall apartment buildings. They summarily evicted all the tenants, using buildings as barracks for their troops and installing their anti-aircraft guns on the roofs in the hope that the greater height would be decisive in bringing the American planes down. This was extremely hard on the poor people who were evicted. With little notice, they had to call on their relatives or friends to accommodate them. I recall that we harboured the elderly Mr and Mrs Segal, close friends of my grandparents, in the covered balcony section of the apartment above the factory in Rue Lafayette, where they lived until the end of the war.

The mounting of these anti-aircraft guns was no more than a cruel farce. The extra height did nothing to achieve the objective and the anti-aircraft shells, which exploded well short of the American planes, caused more deaths from the shrapnel, which sprayed all over the city. As the frequency of the over-flights increased, followed by the futile Japanese response, the danger of windowpanes being shattered from the spraying shrapnel became very real. So we pasted strips of paper all over the windows, in the hope that this would render them shatterproof.

Curfews were imposed and we had to install heavy drapes over the windows to prevent any light being seen from outside. The objective was to prevent the lights of the city from serving as a beacon for night aircrafts. The Japanese organised volunteer street patrols, called 'pao chia' to roam the streets, detecting those who were not adequately 'light proofing' their windows. Heavy sanctions were enforced against violators.

The over-flights of these B-29s substantially increased. Every other day, literally hundreds of these aircrafts flew over Shanghai on their bombing missions. It was like a huge, dark and very noisy cloud passing overhead.

They came in from the interior, as far away as Chunking, on their way to the devastating bombing runs over Tokyo and the other main cities of Japan. I was so terrified by these over-flights that I hid under my bed.

The general talk was that the war was reaching its closing stages. On the 8th May, the news was out that the war in Europe had come to an end with the total defeat of Nazi Germany. The resultant jubilation was tempered by the emerging and horrifying details of the Nazi death and concentration camps, where millions of innocent people, including six million Jews, had been murdered. This information was delivered to us via the Soviet newsreels screened in the Soviet Club. The news was especially tragic for the thousands of Jews from Germany, Austria and Poland, who had found sanctuary in Shanghai, but had left relations back home. As the scale of the atrocities became known, there became little doubt that their loved ones had perished in the Holocaust.

Then on the 17th July, the Hongkew residents were struck by a bombing horror. Although the American focus on specific installations was generally accurate, on that day bombs fell on Hongkew. Many Chinese in the densely populated area died, as well as more than 30 of the Jewish residents. Fortunately this was the only such bombing incident, but it gave everybody an indication of the horror and devastation that would have been caused by a sustained bombing raid.

The Japanese dug in, and more and more troops seemed to enter Shanghai. Everybody sensed that the end was near, but when, nobody knew. Through the Soviet news agency, *Tass*, it was clear that Japan was being very heavily bombed, and that it was hurting. The mood in the streets was getting tense and we were warned not to do anything to antagonise the belligerent Japanese soldiers, who seemed to be everywhere.

When the school year came to a close and the summer holidays began. We were marooned in Shanghai, as we couldn't travel outside the city limits. We played in the laneway leading to the apartment and went to either the Soviet Club or the Jewish Club. And then there was my ubiquitous Hebrew teacher who faithfully turned up several times a week.

With Grandfather no longer with us, there were Grandmother, Tonia and myself occupying apartment twelve. Father, Eva, and Nathan continued to live in apartment eleven. We still met for lunch and dinner, but the atmosphere was gloomy. We missed Grandfather's commanding presence, and the war tensions affected us as well. This atmosphere was aggravated by rumours that the Japanese were going to intern the Russian Jews, who were so far untouched by the Japanese. Uncertainty and apprehension pervaded the air like a thunderstorm about to break.

And then the heavens opened up in early August. In rapid succession we heard that the Soviet Union had declared war on Japan and invaded Manchuria, or Manchuko, as the Japanese had renamed this northern province of China. Their military progress was rapid, as the Japanese were either overwhelmed, or decided not to put up serious resistance. Quickly the Soviet forces captured Harbin, an important centre, where there was still a strong Jewish community.

Rumours swept Shanghai that the Americans had exploded a devastating new bomb on Hiroshima, a major Japanese city. Somehow the word 'atomic bomb' entered the vocabulary as it became clear that this was no ordinary bomb. *Tass*, the Soviet newsagency, began to reveal details of the immense scale of the devastation visited upon Hiroshima, to the extent that we all believed the Japanese could not survive this particular onslaught. They would have to give up. Hope gave way to belief and soon everybody was celebrating the defeat of Japan. People ran out into the streets, hugging each other with joy.

That night, Japanese troops lined most of the main streets with bayonets drawn, but looked impassively at the crowd of revellers. Technically, they were entitled to retaliate against the stupid people taunting them, but they were a disciplined lot and they had been given orders not to take any action. However, the revellers were not to know this and they must have emitted a giant sigh of relief the next morning for not suffering any consequences for their premature celebrations.

The following day felt like a very bad hangover after a raucous party. An uneasy calm descended on Shanghai. There was disbelief that no surrender by Japan had been announced. Nobody was sure what would happen. Naturally, we were not privy to the behind-the-scenes diplomatic activity taking place over the exact terms of the unconditional surrender of Japan, particularly the fate of the emperor, in the aftermath of the surrender.

It took a second atomic bomb, this time over Nagasaki, another major Japanese centre, to convince the Japanese that the Americans meant business, and that the end had really come. Several days later, on the 15th August 1945, came the famous speech of the emperor, announcing the capitulation of Japan and ordering the laying down of arms by the imperial forces. This time the eruption of joy was better founded. Even then, we had to admire the discipline of the Japanese troops, who again had to endure humiliating jeering by a wide cross-section of the population, without taking any action.

Man celebrating VJ Day (Victory over Japan), Sydney 1945

13

CAPITULATION AND PEACE

'History for society is like memory for an individual.
However, it is much more than just possessing
information, for it teaches us lessons, dispels
dangerous myths and, more importantly, helps us to
evaluate the past with perspective.'
Gordon Wood, *The Purpose of The Past*, 2008

Fourteen years after the Japanese first launched their military incursions against a weak Chinese government in 1931, peace finally returned to the world. Germany and Japan were utterly defeated and the task of creating a new world order began.

In Europe, the pre-war political status of nations was largely restored and many nations, particularly in Western Europe, where countries had been occupied by Germany, regained their independence. In Eastern Europe, the reality was somewhat more complicated. Germany was divided into two political entities, and many nations, such as Poland, came under Soviet control, leaving them only nominally sovereign and independent. The Cold War between the Soviet Union and the Western Allies, under the leadership of the United States, imposed a new political landscape in Central and Eastern Europe. The ideological contest between the Soviet Union and the West was already evident during the war, but it had been to the advantage of both sides to play it down, and concentrate instead on defeating Nazi Germany.

In Asia, however, the situation was altogether different. There could be no return to the 'status quo ante' as far as the Europeans were concerned. Japan's military victories in 1941 and 1942, with the attendant humiliation of the European colonial powers, meant that the ethos of traditional European domination could not be sustained, despite the total defeat of Japan. The Japanese, in their early victories, had effectively punctured the aura of invincibility of the European powers, an aura cultivated and developed for over a century. As a result, many of the Dutch, French and British colonies made way for newly independent countries, whilst Japan was forced to give up possession of Korea.

China, under Chiang Kai Shek, was a major beneficiary of Japan's downfall. Not only were Japan's aggressive policies towards it brought to an end, it regained all of the territory that Japan had coveted and captured since 1931. Moreover, the humiliation of extrality, whereby foreigners enjoyed special rights while residing on Chinese territory, was largely abolished. Chiang Kai Shek did an excellent job of selling himself as a hero of the war against Japan. Despite the Chinese suffering enormous losses in lives and territory, they never fully succumbed and their resistance tied down huge Japanese forces, which could have otherwise been deployed against the Allied powers in the Pacific. Britain and America had earlier decided to reward him by abolishing the provisions of the Treaty of Nanking and returning these 'treaty ports' to full Chinese sovereignty. Two anomalies from a past era were allowed to remain - the status of the British colony of Hong Kong and the smaller Portuguese colony of Macau were left undisturbed.

In Shanghai, a new era dawned with the collapse of Japan. The International Settlement and the French Concession were abolished and, for the first time in just over 100 years, the whole of the territory on which Shanghai stood came under total Chinese sovereignty. One mayoral administration would now direct its affairs, rather than the amalgam of several administrations that, before the Japanese occupation, gave it that particular uniqueness.

How the various residents took to this change, naturally depended on who they were. The British, who were interred by the Japanese, had a new legal status. They were now foreigners who no longer enjoyed the benefits of extrality. They would have to adhere to a whole new world of Chinese civil law. Many were very apprehensive about this. But the primary 'raison d'être' of being in Shanghai was to make money, so many decided to stay and see what the future held in store. Similarly, many of the French and other European nationals also stayed to pursue their pre-war interests. Shanghai quickly reverted to its commercial persona and the large pre-war banks, trading and manufacturing corporations, together with their foreign executives and employees, remained to do business.

The position of the Americans improved with the new supremacy of their post-war influence. The effective re-occupation of Shanghai was basically an American affair and that brought in a large number of new civilian and military residents. The citizens of enemy aliens, the Japanese and the Germans, naturally suffered most by the change in fortune, and their influence disappeared.

The Chinese were in a separate category. They were no longer subject to the whims of Japanese brutality, but the poverty of the masses continued unabated. The beggars still filled the streets, rickshaws, that lowest denominator of labour, remained as numerous as ever, and so was the supply of cheap Chinese workers. In fact, much of life in Shanghai continued just as before.

Some of the Jews were profoundly affected by the new era, particularly those who had suffered the most from the war and the Japanese occupation, the refugees from Germany, Austria and Poland who had fled the Nazis and were then incarcerated in run-down Hongkew where they had endured the degradation of a ghetto-like existence. The end of the war was joyously welcomed by them as they were finally free to live where they wanted and to resume their pre-war life, as far as possible. Few of them considered Shanghai home in the way that the Sephardi and Russian Jews did, and most readily took up the visas on offer to the United States, Canada and Australia. The happiness of war's end was naturally marred by the now freely available news of the Holocaust. Most had left family members behind who had hoped to join them, but left it too late. Others had been left behind because they had nowhere to go or they had hoped to tough it out. In any event, the vast majority perished under horrific circumstances. For these refugees to return to their former homes, which had so cruelly spurned them, was akin to settling in a graveyard. New lives had to be built elsewhere.

The Sephardi Jews, who returned to Shanghai from the internment camps, largely carried on as before. They resumed their trading enterprises, confiscated by the Japanese, as well as the rhythm of their pre-war social and Jewish lives. To most of them, Shanghai was home and although they could have moved to other countries, the normalcy which Shanghai settled into, gave little incentive to do so.

The end of the war affected us, the Russian Jews, the least. We were never part of any political process before the war. Living under the rule of the French consul general in the French Concession or the new Chinese administration made little practical difference. As long as we could live safely as Jews, and could continue to earn a comfortable living, we were satisfied. Our self-contained social existence had been undisturbed by the Japanese during their occupation, and we now equally expected that our lives could continue as before.

The non-Jewish Russians who had fled the communist revolution, and who were also largely stateless, were also only mildly affected. Their financial position improved as many found new and lucrative employment with the substantial American military presence in Shanghai. Politically, they were in a quandary. By sentiment, most were opposed to the Soviet regime, which had dispossessed them as a result of the revolution, but they had a genuine attachment to their Russian motherland.

In contrast, to the Jews, historically Russia represented a merciless anti-Semitic country and culture. They were glad to be away from it. As the Russian Jews in Shanghai were largely capitalists from Siberia and Harbin, the new communist regime held no real attraction, even though anti-Semitism had been officially abolished and quite a few Jews were still in the power elite of the regime.

After the end of the war, the Soviet Union issued an amnesty to all Russians in China, inviting all the stateless ones to take up Soviet citizenship, thus entitling them to return to the 'rodina' or motherland. Transport by ship was made available and a number took up this offer and actually returned to the Soviet Union. This turned out to be a mistake for, according to a number of accounts that surfaced later, they were not welcomed back as prodigal children. In fact, they were treated with suspicion, and poorly dealt with, including arrests for treason. It remains a mystery why the Soviet government went to so much effort to entice these people back, only to then treat them so badly.

The Americans were the vanguard of the liberation of Shanghai. Official assumption of authority by the Chinese Kuomingtan forces under Chiang Kai Shek took place, but the visible manifestation of the change was the presence of the American forces. There were a few British and some French troops that also entered Shanghai as part of the liberating forces, but the Americans dominated. I first saw the Americans a few days after Japan's capitulation, in a very low-flying DC3 aeroplane, with its door open and the occupants waving to us. Soon after, they started to swarm in.

To us children, the Americans were wonderful occupiers, gregarious and generous. By then we were starved of chocolates and they gave them away liberally. The most popular chocolates were Mars Bars and we feasted on them. They also introduced us to Wrigley chewing gum in a variety of flavours. They travelled around in jeeps, which we had never seen before, and invited us to hop on for a ride. As it was August and there was no school, we had plenty of time to indulge in all this fun. The American soldiers also offered us cigarettes to direct them to the brothels, and we obliged. We all knew the location of brothels, as Shanghai was full of them. For many of us, this was our first introduction to smoking, and we got hooked. This was all done in secret, of course, as our parents would have been furious.

An autograph-collecting craze somehow started and caught on like wildfire. The idea was to collect as many autographs as possible of American servicemen. Wherever and whenever we saw them, we would accost them and ask for an autograph. We bought special autograph notebooks and they were soon crammed with signatures. What the soldiers must have thought of all of this, I do not know, for they came from a country where only movie stars were badgered for autographs. They seemed happy to oblige, no doubt bemused by all the attention. It did not take long for this deluge of autographs to start to overwhelm us. Quantity started to give way to quality, and we began to be selective. The signatures of privates and corporals were downgraded in favour of higher ranks. Officers' signatures became especially prized, the higher the rank the better. A trade developed among us as to the number of signatures of lower ranks that were equivalent to an officer's signature. We became quite expert in ranking the hierarchy of the American forces and fixed relative values accordingly. The only problem was that officers' autographs were hard to come by. Apart from there being fewer of them, they simply did not wander about the streets or drive jeeps, like enlisted men.

I recall having a real coup with a 'serious' signature. One Friday night we had an officer for Shabbat dinner. He was a purchasing officer with the US army and he contacted Father at the Shanghai Cardboard Box Factory to purchase containers for their army canteen. When my father started to deal with him, he found out that the officer was Jewish and, of course, he invited him home for dinner on Friday night. From the fuss at home that night, it was obvious that we had an important visitor, an officer who would place an important order. In addition, the officer was a Jew, a matter of some wonderment to Russian Jews whose only experience with the military was a very negative one in regard to the tsarist army.

My problem was whether I could ask him for a signature. I knew that Father was anxious that I behave and not be a bother to this special guest. I bided my time, and towards the end of the night, when everyone was merry with food and drink, I sprung the question. The officer was very gracious and agreed to give me not one, but several signatures. I was on top of the world and a real hero to my friends the next day.

The flood of Americans pouring into Shanghai after the war included civilian personnel, executives of the now resumed American enterprises and support personnel for the military. This resulted in the re-opening of the beautiful Shanghai American School, on Avenue Petain, a lovely part of the former French Concession.

American businessmen first opened the school in the early 1900s, to cater to their growing numbers and the children of American missionaries. Well-funded and considered one of the best foreign American schools in the world, it closed down in 1941 as the continuing conflict with the Japanese precipitated an exodus of Americans. It stayed closed right through to the end of the war.

Its re-opening coincided with much discussion at home about my schooling. With the war over, my family was concerned that the Shanghai Jewish School would deteriorate in quality. There had been an exodus of key teachers, and the principal, Mr Kahans, had also resigned. Many of the staff were leaving to take advantage of the readily obtainable visas to the United States, Canada, Australia and other countries. Like many others, Father had also started to worry about the future of Shanghai, given the fundamental change in its political status. Thoughts turned to migrating to the United States and my family felt that attending an American school would prepare me well for such a move. By then, I was an expert at changing schools.

I have good memories of the Shanghai American School. The environment was pleasing as its architecture was modelled on the Cape Cod style of New England. There was a very strong focus on American history, which I found fascinating, and I made many good friends. I was really very happy there. However, this happiness was short-lived as world events again intervened. This time I had to leave, not because I was Jewish, as with the French School, or because of the outbreak of the war in the Pacific, as with the British school, but because of something totally unanticipated - the Cold War. The bitter rivalry that developed between the United States and the Soviet Union, the two major victorious powers of the Second World War, even made its presence felt in far-off Shanghai. Children of parents with Soviet citizenship and all those with Russian surnames were asked to leave the Shanghai American School. The reason given was that the influx of so many American children made it necessary to ask non-Americans to leave, but this was not really convincing. And so, in June 1946, after only ten months, yet another school had to be found. The trouble was that we were running out of options.

The next school selected for me was where my best friend Alex Vinogradov went, St Joan of Arc's College, a boys' school run by the Marist Brothers, a Roman Catholic teaching order from France. It was conveniently located in the same street as the Doumer Apartments. At first, my parents were reluctant to send me to a Roman Catholic school, but there appeared to be little other choice. Despite their reservations, the Marist Brothers proved to be talented and dedicated educators. They were genuinely interested in the welfare of their students, irrespective of their ability to pay the school fees or of their religion. Although they catered to a Roman Catholic, male student body, from lower middle-class families, they were prepared to accept all students who passed their strict standards of conduct and willingness to learn. There were a substantial number of non-Jewish Russian émigré students from poorer backgrounds at the school. To the best of my knowledge, I was the only Jewish boy there.

The main school was a modern and airy structure, next to a classical building, which served as the administrative area. Both buildings faced a large sports field along Avenue Joffre, the main thoroughfare of the French Concession. The school had a French section where all classes were taught in French to prepare the students for the entrance examinations for the Sorbonne University in Paris. I was in the English speaking section, which prepared us for the entrance examinations for Cambridge University. We also had to study French and we were expected to speak it well. A wide variety of subjects were compulsory: Mathematics, Sciences, Literature, Geography and History were all taught with equal emphasis. Predictably, Religious Education was also compulsory. Every morning, before classes began, we had to stand up and recite the 'Our Father' and the 'Hail Mary'. Catholics were expected to cross themselves, but this was not insisted upon for boys of other religions. Attendance at the chapel attached to the school was encouraged, but wasn't mandatory for those of other faiths. To pass the year, however, all students had to sit the exams for the religious subjects.

The school frequently sent home reports, covering conduct, tests, our attendance and our final exam results. The system was designed to keep control over the students' progress, before things got out of hand. Naughtiness was not tolerated, and was punished by caning, either on the palm of the hand, for minor incidents, or on the buttocks for serous offences. The Brothers certainly brooked no nonsense from the students.

Sport was also a high priority and the school's spacious grounds provided ample opportunity for a variety of sports to be played. Football, or soccer, was very popular and, curiously, so was softball. The Brothers encouraged us to have hobbies and other interests and they were prepared to put in the effort to nurture them. One of the Brothers introduced Alex and I to photography. The school had a darkroom in an old shed, which contained a stack of old Lumiere glass photographic plates and a camera, into which these plates were loaded. Often, after school, we would rush over to develop the plates and print them. Alex and I spent hours there together, learning about chemicals for developing, fixing and printing photos.

From July 1946, and for the next three years, on most mornings Alex and I would walk together to school. This took only a few minutes, which was fortunate in winter when it was cold and often rainy. On the way home, we would buy pickled mangoes, prunes and other Chinese delicacies from the old man who ran a 'tuck-shop' from his cart, just outside the school grounds.

In summer, during the months of July and August, the Brothers opened up the school for games and activities. Going away during the summer holidays was not common; during the war it had been impossible to travel, while after the war, the resorts were quite far away and expensive. So we wandered back to school for pool games, chess and sporting activities, supervised by the Brothers.

With the war over, restrictions on foreign films were lifted, and there was a veritable flood of American films. Initially, many of the pre-war movies were resurrected and shown. Then came the more current ones. After the wartime drought, our appetite for these American films was insatiable. We would see anything. Shanghai was full of cinemas and we were particularly lucky to have one in Rue Doumer, virtually opposite the lane entrance to our building. On some Saturdays and Sundays we would go to several sessions on the same day, starting out at the Doumer Cinema in the morning and ending up at the nearby Cathay Cinema. There was also a deluge of American comic books. We were avid readers of these new comic books, which were quite different from the English Biggles-style comic books that we read before the war. Our parents were against us reading them; they felt that we would never read serious books if we got hooked on this type of undemanding literature.

Our other favourite weekend pastime was to have a picnic in one of the nearby parks or afternoon tea at the Bridge Garden on the Whampoo

River, followed by a short boat ride to see the various foreign warships in port. Then I would head over to Betar to practice formation marching and throwing grenades, using round stones. Looking back, it seems bizarre, but we had a lot of fun practising at liberating Palestine from the British.

My social life was basically divided into two. My school was for boys only and the students came from a very wide non-Jewish milieu, mainly Catholic and White Russian. Many of the Catholic boys came from mixed parentage - 'half-caste', as we unkindly called them. They were generally children of Macau Portuguese and Chinese parents who produced particularly good-looking girls. We would always try to mingle with the boys who had sisters, so as to meet them. I encountered very little anti-Semitism from this crowd. The worst would be epithets like 'dirty Jew', but never any physical threats. The Betar crowd, on the other hand, was totally Russian Jewish and thus ethnically very homogeneous. As a result, the friendships were comfortable and unthreatening. Betar was open to both boys and girls, so the dynamics were different, less rough and with generally more serious conversation. I seemed to move between these two disparate social circles quite well, which stood me in good stead for later in life.

St Joan of Arc's College. Brother Gilbert on far left

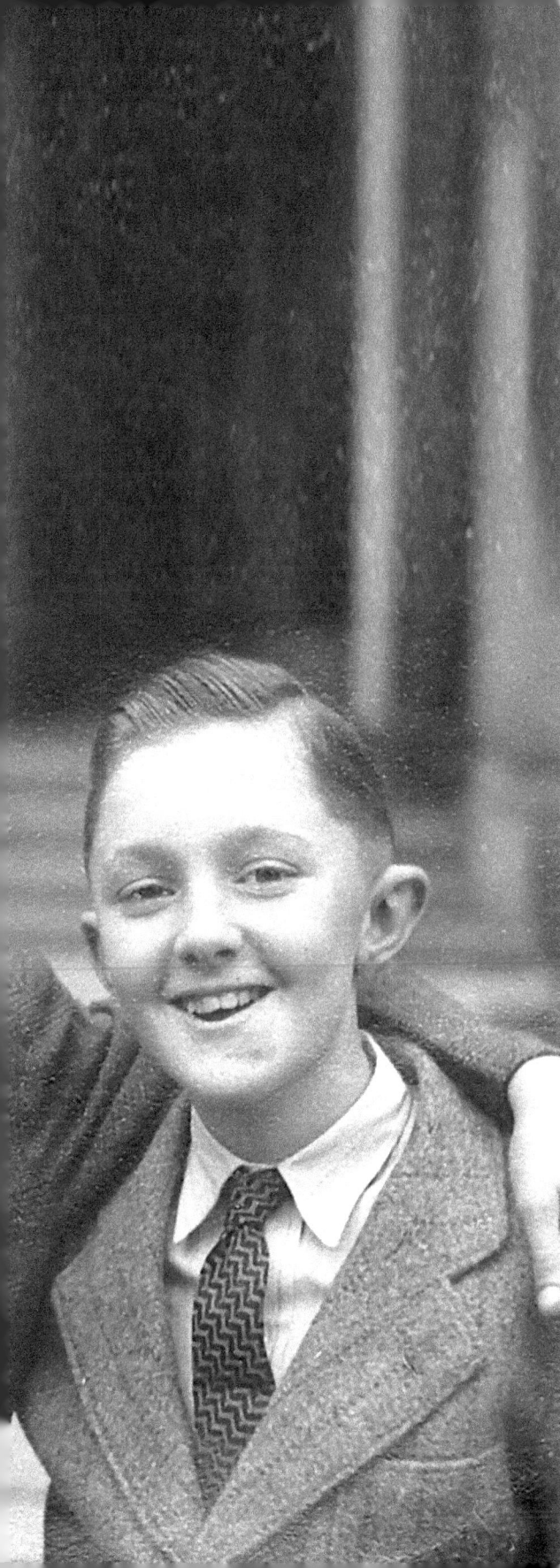
With Leo Kalageorgi
and Alex, 1946

COLLÈGE S^{TE} JEANNE D'ARC

JUNIOR CERTIFICATE

This is to certify that __S. Moshinsky__
satisfied the College Authorities in the compulsory
subjects: English Language, Elementary Mathematics, and
French and in the following sections:

History & Geography, Trigonometry,
Additional Mathematics

Shanghai, August 7th 1949   Principal

Bro. R. Albert

In a US navy hat,1947

With Elijah and Nathan, 1946

14

POST-WAR SHANGHAI

*'My friends and I had to learn how to live in a dual
currency environment. When given our pocket
money, we immediately went into one of the many
money shops and exchanged it for American dollars.'*
Sam

The first full year of peace, 1946, saw another addition to the family. On the 7th January 1946, Elijah was born. I recall being taken to see Eva and the baby in the Eden Hospital, a spacious and luxurious establishment. They came straight home to the Doumer Apartments from the hospital.

By the middle of 1946, the American military presence started to wane and gradually Chinese authority began to assert itself. At first, some of the street names began to change. This was the second time that we had to get used to new street names, as the Japanese and their Chinese collaborators had already changed the name of many streets once before. Poverty among the Chinese was still widespread, despite the general business prosperity. It was the change to our currency that we noticed the most. It had been standardised to the Chinese yuan and most prices were being expressed in it. The true value of the Chinese yuan was measured against the exchange rate to the United States dollar, the new international currency standard.

The Chinese government started to mismanage the economy and serious corruption was becoming a reality. The head of the government was Generalissimo (as he liked to call himself) Chiang Kai Shek, but the powerful Soong family really dominated the running of the country. Chiang Kai Shek was married to one of the Soong sisters and their web of influence was very strong. Before long, serious inflation started to take hold and had a disastrous effect on the economy. Prices, in terms of the Chinese yuan, started to escalate and had a corresponding impact on the exchange rate vis-a-vis the American dollar. To preserve purchasing power, we could not hold currency in the yuan, as within a short period we would have to pay more yuan for the very same article. Then the rate of inflation escalated and this affected all items, including staples such as rice and bread. This had a terribly corrosive effect on the economy.

The way that some people protected themselves from the inflationary spiral was to exchange their yuan holding into American dollars and to re-exchange small amounts back into yuan, only as necessary. To facilitate this, small money exchange shops opened up everywhere. But not everybody understood this system or had the means to do it. The average wage earner was paid a monthly salary in Chinese yuan, and saw most of its purchasing power eroded within days. The resultant suffering was great, and was soon accompanied by widespread industrial unrest. All of this started to sound the death knell for the nationalist regime.

From a relatively early age, my friends and I had to learn how to live in a dual currency environment. When given our pocket money, we immediately went into one of the many money shops and exchanged it for American dollars. We had to be continually appraised of the current exchange rate, which we obtained from street moneychangers. The situation got so out of hand that the exchange rate descended into the hundreds of thousands, and even the millions. This was all too reminiscent of the extreme inflationary period in Germany which raged from 1920 to 1923, when wheelbarrows were needed to carry money.

The situation became so untenable that in 1948 the by then discredited government introduced a new currency - the gold yuan. It was officially pegged at four gold yuans to the American dollar and this had to be backed by gold and silver, which everybody was exhorted to surrender to the government. All prices were reset in terms of this new currency and punitive measures were threatened if any violations were exposed. In fact, a number of people were openly shot for non-compliance, but this did little to give solidity to the new currency.

At the head table with Eva and Grandmother
The only photo from the Barmitzvah

15

MY BARMITZVAH
AND THE SUMMER OF '47

'Keep your mind busy to accomplish things.
Keep your mind open to understand things.'
Ancient Chinese wisdom

My Barmitzvah was celebrated on Saturday the 8th July 1947, the day corresponding to the 20th day of the Hebrew month of Tammuz, my birthday. The world, and Shanghai, had changed dramatically in the thirteen years since my birth. The Japanese, who had initiated the hostilities against China in 1931, had surrendered unconditionally in 1945. Nazi Germany had come to power and then capitulated, leaving a legacy of unprecedented human suffering, including the genocide of six million Jews. The key wartime allies, the United States, Great Britain and the Soviet Union, were now locked into an ideological conflict, known as the Cold War. In China, a new conflict was emerging between the incumbent government, the nationalists led by Chiang Kai Shek, and a communist-led rebellion in the north led by Mao Tse Tung, then still a relatively unknown name.

A year earlier, in preparation for my Barmitzvah, my Hebrew teacher had shifted emphasis to the learning of my 'parasha'. In the Orthodox tradition, I had to learn to chant the relevant parasha and the 'haftorah', as well as the customary blessings.

Shortly before the big day, the question of a new suit arose. I had never owned a suit. Any clothes I had needed were purchased off the rack from the shops in Avenue Joffre or at one of the big department stores in Nanking Road. But for this special occasion, it was decided that Father's personal tailor should measure me up for a hand-made suit and some matching shirts. Several fittings later, in the tailor's workshop, Grandmother was finally satisfied with my Barmitzah outfit.

This was the beginning of a tradition that lasted right up until I left Shanghai. Every few years, I would go with Father to the tailor, to be fitted for new suits, trousers, sports jackets and shirts. The only items purchased ready-made were underwear, handkerchiefs and the odd hat. In the year following my Barmitzvah, Father decided that even my shoes should be hand-made. His friend Mr Kaufman was a leather merchant, who took us to several tanneries to select the leather for both summer and winter shoes. We then proceeded to his shoemaker for fittings. Father always took pride in his appearance. Sometimes I would accompany him to his barber, also in Avenue Joffre, where he would have a haircut, a shave and a manicure. Outside, his personal rickshaw would be waiting to take him to the factory.

My Barmitzvah ceremony was held in The New Synagogue in Route Tenant de la Tour. There was a big crowd, including all my friends from Betar and from school. I performed quite well and when I finished, the ladies and girls in the upstairs gallery threw sweets from the balcony. Rabbi Ashkenazi said a few words of congratulations at the conclusion of what felt like a very long morning.

After the service, there was a large kiddush in the vestibule of the synagogue. Then, those invited for lunch walked around the corner to the Jewish Club on Rue Pichon, where the festivities continued. It was a very hot day and the lunch was held in the lovely front room of the club. There were no speeches at the lunch, only a few toasts in my honour as well as the customary blessings.

After dessert and the prayers, my friends and I rushed out to play in the spacious grounds of the Jewish Club. We played soccer and hide and seek. By late afternoon, everybody was exhausted and I went home to open my presents.

Although a long and exciting day, I very much missed my father who was away on a business trip to the United States. It was customary for a father to accompany his son to the 'bima' for the Torah readings and this had occurred at all the Barmitzvahs I had been to. With Grandfather having already passed away, I felt very much alone being the only Moshinsky male standing on the bima.

It was explained to me that Father's trip to the United States was unavoidable. Apparently, by the beginning of 1947, serious doubts were developing as to the future of Shanghai as a commercial centre and as a home for people like us. It was clear that the Chinese were making a big mess of running the place. There was widespread corruption, growing inflation and the emergence of open lawlessness. With my grandmother's family, the Caismans, now settled in Chicago, Father decided to go over and assess the possibilities of transferring our family's business to the US, the preferred destination of everyone contemplating leaving China.

I am sure that he did not intend to be away for this special day. Yet, transport in this chaotic post-war period was still hard to obtain. A berth on a ship going to the United States came up at short notice and Father decided to take it. I was told that he would make it up to me upon his return. I believed this, but his absence still left a palpable void. I was disappointed that he was not there to share the experience with me.

Father returned from America shortly after my Barmitzvah. At the time I wasn't sure what he had accomplished, but we were not about to pack our bags to leave Shanghai. I was happy to see that, as promised, he came back laden with gifts. He brought a lot of lovely clothes for Eva and Grandmother, and baby toys for Nathan and Elijah. For me he brought the new and fashionable clothes that American teenagers wore, which were still not available in the Shanghai shops. I also got a Parker pen set, then a standard American Barmitzvah present, and a gold-plated safety razor, both of which I cherished for a long time. With my new clothes and possessions, I was the envy of my friends.

For us all, he brought back the latest automatic record player, which could stack and play up to half a dozen records at a time. We used to stand around it and watch in awe as the needle hand automatically rose up at the end of the record and the next record fell in place. Then this clever needle hand gently lowered itself into exactly the right position to start at the beginning of the new record.

Father had also spent some time in New York, with its large Jewish community, so he brought back some Jewish records - music and comedy. Until then, we only had a few scratchy old records of Chaliapin, a noted Russian singer, and some cantors singing liturgical melodies. The new American Jewish comedy records caused a sensation. The record about a Jewish tailor called Sam, who made the pants too long, kept us all enthralled. We also loved another record about a Barmitzvah boy who received so many pens that in his speech he introduced himself as a fountain pen. Our friends visited us over many evenings to admire the record player and to enjoy the records.

Soon after his return, Father decided to purchase a motorcar. I am not sure why. I suspect that his peers in the business world had them and he felt that it was important for his prestige. Much to the disgust of Grandmother and Eva, who thought it unnecessary and extravagant, he purchased a black Studebaker, a fashionable car in those days. It came with a full-time driver who kept it clean and shiny. The problem in Shanghai was that the car was more of a hindrance than an aid. The streets were very congested and the rickshaws were more adept at weaving in and out of the traffic. We used to laugh that it took twice as long to get to the factory by car than by rickshaw. On Sunday afternoons, we would be taken for drives around the city, sometimes stopping at a park. But most of the time, the car was standing outside the Doumer Apartments or the factory, with the Chinese chauffer continuously washing and polishing it. After about a year, Father decided to get rid of the Studebaker and he turned to pedicabs, which were coming into vogue.

The summer of 1947 was spent in Shanghai. My life followed a rhythm. Every morning I went to the summer program at St Joan of Arc's, and in the afternoons I went to Betar. The program at Betar was becoming increasingly political, centring on the issue of Palestine and the creation of a Jewish State. We were taught the history of Zionism, with a very strong emphasis on the teachings and philosophy of the charismatic Vladimir Jabotinsky and his successor, Menahim Begin, who established and headed a breakaway group from the military wing of the establishment Zionists, called Irgun Zvai Leumi. The Irgun pursued a more aggressive resistance policy against the British Mandate authorities, as well as the Arab militants who were waging increasing attacks on the Jews of Palestine. The Betar movement strongly identified itself with the Irgun and the activities were focused on physical fitness and military discipline.

All this Zionist activity, which was also engaged in by the adults in the Jewish Club, came to a head in November 1947 when the United

Nations, meeting in New York, decided to take a vote on the partition of Palestine. This followed Britain's decision to abandon the mandate, which was awarded to it by the League of Nations at the Versailles Peace Conference, following the Allied victory in World War One. A positive vote for partition entailed the creation of a Jewish state alongside a Palestinian state, with Jerusalem, the city coveted by both sides of the conflict, to become an international city. Neither of the sides to the conflict was particularly happy with the partition plan, least of all the revisionist movement, which still adhered to the concept of a Jewish State on both banks of the Jordan River. But the Zionist movement and the Jewish people as a whole reconciled themselves to the partition plan as the next best opportunity available for the creation of a much-desired Jewish state. So the successful outcome of the United Nations vote was crucial and we all followed, with baited breath, the course of the voting in far-off New York. We were all tuned into the short wave radio as the various nations cast their votes and the leaders tallied them. There was much excitement and we were all infected by it. When the final votes counted resulted in a majority for the partition plan, a loud roar erupted and we all went out in the cold of a Shanghai November to dance the 'horah' and sing the 'Hatikvah'.

A photo of Abe posted to Grandmother from America.

To Mother
[signature]

Betar, 1947. Far right

Photo taken by me from my bedroom window in Moganshan, 1948

16

HOLIDAY IN MOGANSHAN

'We live in the present, we dream of the future and
we learn eternal truths from the past.'
Chiang Kai Shek

In July 1948, the family decided to spend the summer break in Moganshan, a summer resort in the mountains, some distance from Shanghai. This involved catching a train for a two-hour ride to Hangchow, now called Hangzu, a pretty town on the edge of the beautiful West Lake. From Hangchow, we travelled by bus to the mountain resort's central bus station. Then we partly walked and were partly carried up by coolies to the villa. We stayed in Moganshan until the end of August to avoid the oppressive heat of Shanghai. Many of my parents' friends also decided to have their holidays there, including the Vinogradovs. It was a wonderful holiday. There was a swimming pool and Alex and I used to swim for hours. My father and his friends would spend the day playing cards and the women played mah-jong, a popular Chinese game played with ivory tiles. In the evenings we all visited each other's villas. I had my own room on the top floor of the three-storey solid stone house we rented and I loved waking up early to observe and take photographs of the beautiful scenery and stunning sunrises.

The Moganshan holiday was the reason I gave up eating chicken for life. That year, it was the only form of meat available. So we had eggs for breakfast, and chicken for every other meal, in almost every form - boiled, fried, minced, and, of course, Friday night chicken soup. I was so fed up with this food regime that I swore that I would give up eating chicken forever.

Moganshan was also the favourite summer resting place of the ruler of China, Generalissimo Chiang Kai Shek, and he had a large house there. One morning, when we were on one of our many mountain trail walks, military personnel suddenly appeared and ordered us to a side track, as the Generalissimo and Madam Chiang Kai Shek were taking a stroll. I managed to catch a glimpse of him. He was walking with the help of a stick and appeared frail. Obviously he was weighed down by the unfavourable course of the civil war against the communist forces led by Mao Tse Tung. Within a year, his reign over mainland China would collapse and he would flee with his entourage and supporters to the island of Taiwan to live out the rest of his life.

Father and friend relaxing in Moganshan

The Shanghai Racecourse, vilified by the communists
as a symbol of western capitalist decadence

17

THE BEGINNING OF THE END

*'Politics is war without bloodshed, while war is
politics with bloodshed.'*
Mao Tse Tung

Our return to Shanghai from Moganshan, at the end of August 1948, heralded the end of Shanghai as we knew it, as the political and military position of the nationalist government began to suffer evident deterioration. The communist forces, under the command of Mao Tse Tung, had started to gain control of the conflict over the forces loyal to Chiang Kai Shek. The entry of the Soviet Union in the war against the Japanese, in August 1945, resulted in the bringing of Manchuria, renamed Manchukuo by the Japanese, under communist rule. From that vantage point, the Soviet Union was in a better position to provide support to the communist forces, which were holed up in the caves of Yenan, and this, in turn, provided them with the opportunity to break out of there. Their hibernation during the war against the Japanese provided them with the opportunity to refine their political philosophy and their military discipline. Although the support of the Soviet Union was important for their emergence as the contender for governing China, it was really the failure of the moral and political attitudes and practices of the nationalist government that provided them with their primary opportunity.

In my last year at St Joan of Arc's College, from September 1948 to May 1949, when the communist forces entered Shanghai, the decline of nearly all aspects of governmental administration was evident. Of primary importance was the collapse of the gold yuan, introduced just over a year earlier, as a major initiative to stabilise the exchange rate to the American dollar. In June 1949, when the nationalist forces were already driven to Canton, in the south of China, just before they decamped to Taiwan, the exchange rate was quoted in the hundreds of millions to the American dollar. Obviously, this wreaked havoc for the millions who worked for a fixed wage, paid in Chinese currency and who did not have the access or the expertise to change their wages into the American dollar and back.

There was much industrial unrest and municipal services, such as garbage collection, suffered. The streets were full of uncollected refuse, and we had to walk with handkerchiefs pressed to our noses, so terrible was the stench. Law enforcement had also broken down, and the nights were particularly dangerous. In fact, all the residents living in the lane that serviced the Doumer Apartments and the other villas got together and had a huge wooden gate and a small guardhouse erected, which was manned around the clock. Access was by a small entrance in the big gate, after identification by the guard. I had just started to go to parties and to come home late at night. I had to bang loudly on the gate to wake the watchman and shout my name in Chinese, which was 'Sho Mo' so that he would let me in. Often Grandmother or Tonia would stay up to make sure that I got home safely.

The streets had even more beggars than before and the sight of mothers with their hungry babies, many literally dying of hunger, was most distressing. There was also something new in the horrors we had to encounter: the streets had become full of maimed soldiers in tattered uniforms with exposed bloody limbs, adding to the already large beggar population. The policy of the nationalist army was to discharge its soldiers who became wounded in battle, as they were no longer of any use.

The foreign community watched the civil war with increasing consternation, particularly as the nationalists vowed to defend Shanghai 'to the last man'. Sandbagged pillboxes were erected at the major intersections and the city started to take on a beleaguered atmosphere. The civil war was waging north of the Yangtze River but many felt that it was too wide to be breached. We all hoped that perhaps the communists would entrench themselves north of the Yangtze and the nationalists to the south, thus saving Shanghai from the communists. But after the communists fired at a British frigate on the Yangtze River on the 20th April 1949 in the celebrated 'Amethyst Incident', most people felt that the nationalists were doomed, irrespective of the width of the Yangtze. A few days later, the communist forces achieved the inconceivable and actually crossed the river in great force.

It then became a matter of time before flight from Shanghai became a priority. Many of my friends were starting to leave and the parties I was invited to were increasingly becoming farewell parties.

On the 24th May 1949, the communist army marched into Shanghai, without any fanfare. Despite the promise to defend the city, the nationalists seemed to melt away one night. Shanghai fell without as much as a single shot being fired. Father took Eva and me for a walk along Avenue Joffre one late afternoon to watch the communist army marching down the street. We were struck by how many wore American uniforms and the amount of American equipment they had, including jeeps and trucks. Apparently as items of American military aid were being given to the nationalists, their corrupt generals would on-sell them to the communists.

With this peaceful filing of soldiers, taking over one of the great cities of the world, Shanghai's destiny changed even more drastically than when the Japanese took over the foreign concessions on the 7th December 1941. Back then, somehow, a vestige of the old life continued. Apart from the takeover of the assets of enemy aliens, under the Japanese, the capitalist fabric of Shanghai was basically left unchanged. As Japan's war economy needed many of the products of Shanghai's large manufacturing industry, property rights were respected and real estate trade had continued.

The communist takeover drastically changed all of this. Firstly, its philosophy was rooted in the abolition of privately owned property in favour of state ownership and central direction of economic activity. This eliminated the raison d'être of virtually all non-Chinese, as well as many Chinese businessmen, together with their vast retinue of executives and other employees. Secondly, the communist takeover of Shanghai, as well as the rest of China, sought to expunge, once and for all, the vestiges of the foreign presence associated with national humiliation and exploitation. And so the die was cast for the complete makeover of Shanghai.

To the credit of the new communist authorities, their first priorities were to deal with the fundamental ills of Shanghai, particularly those caused by the terrible incompetence of the nationalist government. A new currency was introduced, which was not linked to an exchange rate with a foreign currency. The new authorities did something that was unheard of: they established a price structure for all items, particularly the daily staples, following the creation of the new 'peoples' currency'. Miraculously the inflationary spiral that had plagued the Chinese masses was brought to an abrupt end. They then set about organising the labour force into 'patriotic brigades', and they abolished 'anti-social' strikes. Following this, the city started to function as it should. The mountains of garbage were cleaned up and the beggars were removed.

When the authorities announced their intention to tackle the city's numerous and notorious flies, many received the news with scepticism, if not derision. But they did it! By the time I left Shanghai in September 1951, there was scarcely a fly to be seen. How was all this accomplished, and so quickly?

Firstly, the Chinese population had become sick and tired of nationalist corruption and mismanagement. The promise of order and stability had a powerful appeal. The communists were also very able communicators. One of the first things they did was to string loudspeakers in the trees of the main streets, all connected to a central broadcasting source, which continuously blared forth messages on all sort of subjects, including the campaign to eradicate the flies. It started off as a social message - it was the patriotic duty of everybody to maintain a minimum standard of hygiene and also to kill as many flies as possible. Later, incentives were introduced. Levels of 'heroes' were designated, depending on how many flies were personally killed. These heroes were publicly recognised and lauded through the loudspeakers and the newly controlled newspapers, which were pasted on to prominent billboards throughout the city. Poverty was no barrier to being kept informed as to one's social responsibilities. The communists were also committed to the elimination of hunger. Everyone was put to work and promised at least a bowl of rice a day. This was a very powerful mechanism for cementing support of the broad masses to the new regime.

There were also powerful sanctions against the recalcitrant. They were labelled 'enemies of the people', bent on frustrating the onward march of the collective wellbeing of the nation. To reinforce the message, large trials were held at the Shanghai Racecourse, which the communists vilified as a symbol of western capitalist decadence. The stands were filled to capacity and the unfortunate people, who were caught disregarding regulations or engaging in anti-governmental activities, were arraigned in the middle of the grounds. A communist party official then read out the charges on the loudspeakers and the thousands of people assembled in the stands were invited to express their verdict. There were no opportunities to contest these charges and, after the multitude invariably shouted 'guilty', the accused would generally be executed on the spot, 'in accordance with the will of the people.'

In addition, the communist leadership was very effective in dealing with the many social ills of the city. The partaking of opium was banned and the many dens were summarily closed. How the many thousands of addicts were medically dealt with, I do not know, but they simply disappeared. Finally, after 150 years, the Chinese were rid of the scourge of opium. Similarly with prostitution, the multitudes of brothels were closed down and the prostitutes were put to more gainful employment. What Christian missionaries were unable to achieve for decades had also been successfully accomplished. Another important achievement of the new Chinese rulers was the standardisation of language. The northern dialect, Mandarin, was adopted as the new national language. Gone also was the proliferation of regional dialects which had divided the Chinese people since time immemorial. With this came a campaign of literacy and, here again, there was success.

But for us, the foreigners, this was a difficult situation. The American support of the Chiang Kai Shek regime turned the United States, and all westerners, into enemies, who were constantly vilified. American and western films were banned, as were their newspapers and other publications. Even our beloved comic books disappeared. The hegemony of the west was being gradually eradicated and Shanghai started to lose its distinctly cosmopolitan atmosphere, in favour of a pronounced Chinese identity. Foreigners were made to feel that there was no future for them and many more started to leave as the rationale for their existence became eroded.

St Francis Xavier's College, middle row.

18

SCHOOL IN HONGKEW

'Physics requires the power of reasoning, while miracles demand the gift of faith.'
Brother Kevin of St Francis Xavier's College

It was against this unpromising background that I commenced my final two years of schooling at St Francis Xavier's College in Hongkew, in September 1949, having graduated from St Joan of Arc's.

St Francis Xavier's College was one of the oldest schools in China, having been established by the Jesuits, an elite Roman Catholic order of priests in 1874. The running of the school was eventually taken over by the Marist Brothers, the same teaching order that ran St Joan of Arc's. The teaching program was extremely rigorous and the discipline was equally strict. A comprehensive curriculum of subjects was mandatory, irrespective of personal inclination. The philosophy of the Brothers was to prepare students for a difficult future by exposing them to the entire spectrum of education. The compulsory subjects also included three religion subjects.

The standard in these subjects was geared to the passing of the senior Cambridge University entry examinations. We were tested weekly in every subject and our marks were included in our weekly reports, which had to be signed off by a parent. The school was equipped with a good Physics and Chemistry laboratory and there was also strong emphasis placed on a variety of sports. All in all, it was an extremely demanding and, to me, satisfying educational regime.

I recall those years fondly and with gratitude. I developed a very good rapport with a number of the Brothers, with whom I would spend time after class discussing the lessons further. Surprisingly, for the only Jewish boy in the school, I was interested in and performed well in all of the religion subjects. I did not feel any anti-Semitism, although I sometimes took exception to the lurid descriptions of certain religious teachings. For example, in the Gospel of St Matthew, which was the set piece for those years, the scene describing Jesus chasing the money-changers from the Temple was, in my opinion, objectionable. The overall picture conveyed was that a Jewish place of worship was degrading and offensively materialistic, compared with the piety of a Christian church. After class, I expressed my objection to the Brother. The fact that I felt free to do so was a reflection of the atmosphere at the school. In fact, rather than take issue with my raising the matter, the Brother was visibly pleased that a student was attentive and interested enough to engage him further in the class lessons. Many of the Catholic boys were really not interested in the religion portion of their education. As soon as the bell rang, they would be out like a shot.

One of the most abiding concepts that the Brothers left me with was that of faith. One day, after a morning of Physics and Catechism classes, I asked the Brother how he could reconcile the rationality of physics with such beliefs as the 'Immaculate Conception' of the Virgin Mary and the 'Ascension' of Jesus Christ to heaven. He replied, without any sense of hesitation, that the former required the power of reasoning, whilst the latter demanded the gift of faith. He then went on to explain the concept of faith and how it was needed in a personal belief system, as not all aspects of life could be resolved through the process of scientific and rational reasoning. Soon I came to appreciate this, and it has helped me come to terms with many subsequent events in my life.

For students living in the former French Concession, the school was quite far away. Alex and I had to set off early in the morning to get there on time and we often came home quite late. We travelled by public transport on trams and buses, which were generally very crowded with Chinese people.

Travelling to school in those years was quite exciting and even dangerous. By the beginning of 1950, the civil war between the nationalists, by then holed up in Taiwan and the communists, now in control of the whole of the Chinese mainland, burst into aerial warfare, some of it over Shanghai. Often, on the way to school, and even while we were at school, sirens would sound and anti-aircraft gunfire would soon follow. This was not long after the Korean War broke out, when the North Koreans, supported by the Soviet Union and communist China, invaded South Korea, then under American protection. The war rapidly escalated when the American forces, under the legendary General Macarthur, invaded Korea and pushed the North Korean forces right back to the Chinese border. This, in turn, brought communist China directly into the Korean War. All this heightened the tense atmosphere in Shanghai. Nobody knew how we would be affected, particularly as there was talk that the Americans would bomb China, possibly even with atomic bombs. The Soviet Union and China, who had till now been ideological allies, now became military ones as well.

A detachment of the Soviet air force was stationed in and around Shanghai. We started to see Russian airmen walking the streets and there was much curiosity surrounding their presence. The differences between when the American forces entered Shanghai, way back in August 1945, and these Russians in 1950, could not have been greater. There was no friendly fraternisation with the Russian airmen, even though so many of us were of Russian origin. The Russians kept to themselves and did not encourage us to get close to them. Certainly there was no chasing after autographs, chocolates, cigarettes or rides on jeeps. They were never invited to our homes and the question of whether any of them were Jewish was never discussed. What we did observe and remark on was that these Russians were spending all their pay buying up everything they saw. This was surprising to us, as by then the months of communist rule had emptied the shops of nearly all of the lavish merchandise that Shanghai was known for. It was clear that what was deprivation to us was still plenty to them. It was, indeed, an eye opener.

The first year of Chinese communist rule in Shanghai was relatively benign. The immediate effect was the curtailment of western culture: American and British films, comic books, and many items of imported merchandise disappeared, resulting in the gradual depletion of the once bountiful Shanghai stores. An element of censorship was introduced. The main English language newspaper, the *North China Daily News* which had reopened following Japan's defeat in 1945, was forced to close again as did a number of foreign language radio stations which stopped broadcasting. But against this was the evident improvement of many aspects of civil life.

The Jewish Club continued to function, as did our Betar group, admittedly on a gradually reduced level as the emigration of foreigners gathered pace. It was the end of the Shanghai we knew, although many still hoped the communist authorities would not be able to digest this huge metropolis and it would somehow escape its seeming inevitable fate. This was not to be.

In the second year of communist rule, the pressure on the remnants of the foreign presence accelerated. The exodus of expatriates produced inevitable results: the foreign banks and insurance companies departed, the foreign clubs and schools also closed down, as patronage, teachers and students dwindled. The businesses that remained began to get 'investigatory' calls from the authorities.

One such call was to our family business. The Shanghai Cardboard Box Factory had managed to maintain normal manufacturing operations since its inception. One day, a number of cadres, officials of the new communist regime, called and politely asked to examine the accounting records of the business. Supposedly it was to assess whether anything illegal was taking place. At this stage, it was permissible to still carry on business. As Father recounted it, although no illegal operations were found, the examiners noted that over the years no income taxes had been paid. My father pointed out, through interpreters, that all existing municipal taxes had been properly paid, but that no income taxes had been paid because there were none in force. The investigators were still not satisfied, explaining that this non-payment of income taxes over the years amounted to an exploitation of the workers, who were Chinese. The fact that for so many years the business voluntarily housed and fed a number of key workers made no impression. They took the figures, which they had gleaned from the records, and said that they would be back.

In due course the communist officials did return, with their verdict. They levied an enormous figure, which, of course, the business could not pay. A process of extended negotiations took place to resolve how the business could discharge this arbitrarily assessed tax owing to the Shanghai People's Government. The business, with its substantial stock of machinery, cardboard and printing inks, not to speak of the goodwill associated with having been in operation since the early 1930s, became virtually worthless overnight. Anyway, who would outlay the substantial amount that the business would normally be worth, in this new business environment?

Why the communists did not confiscate the business outright, I do not know. Instead a tedious legal process was undertaken, which resulted in the same end: the business was ultimately taken over by the state for non-payment of the newly levied taxes. There was also a symbolic interim step, as it was deemed that a foreigner could not employ Chinese workers. So Wang Tu Tsai, the loyal and trusted manager for so many years, was vested with the running of the Shanghai Cardboard Box Factory, on behalf of the people. These handover negotiations for the factory, as well as for the four other properties we owned, would last two years. I received special permission to leave earlier, but it was not until early 1952 that Father was finally granted exit visas for himself and the rest of the family to leave China.

These events reinforced the fact that there could be no future for us and other foreigners in the new China. Being communist, the regime was ideologically opposed to the concept of private capitalism. Just like in the Soviet Union, and the other communist states of Eastern Europe, all economic activities would progressively be conducted by the state. Furthermore, this Chinese government was determined to eradicate the influence and position of the foreigner, regarded as the symbol of Chinese humiliation and servitude for over a century. So the foreigners, who were primarily European, but also Japanese and Indian, gradually found that their place in Shanghai, and the rest of China, had eroded to the point where they had to emigrate. The authorities encouraged this process.

The problem for many, including our family, was where to go. The British, Americans, and nationals of various other countries were in possession of passports entitling them to return to their respective countries, or to travel to any other country that would have them. Even the Japanese had a homeland to return to, albeit devastated as a result of American bombing. But many foreigners were, like us, genuinely stateless; that is, not a national of any country. What had been an advantage during the war, in that we could not be classified as enemy aliens and, therefore, not be subject to internment, now turned out to be a great disadvantage. There were some options, but none of them palatable. There were representatives of several South American countries in Shanghai who were prepared to sell visas for money. But these were unknown and questionable destinations. The

Philippine government, through the offices of the United Nations and a very caring local Philippine consul, was prepared to set aside a portion of an island for transit purposes, until the eventual destinations were established. Some foreigners took up this option but the facilities there turned out to be primitive. A number of rich Chinese entrepreneurs were able to bribe their way to Hong Kong, where many of them eventually became very successful.

The stateless Russian Jews like our family, possessed visas to go to the state of Israel, newly established in May 1948. These visas had been recently issued by Moshe Yuval, Israel's vice consul in New York who came to Shanghai specifically for that purpose. A good proportion of the community did choose this avenue and most were eventually able to establish comfortable lives there. But initially it was very hard for them. Their early letters described the difficult conditions that new immigrants were subjected to. There was a lack of accommodation, food and work opportunities. Despite our Zionist leanings, we were reluctant to endure such hardships.

For the more comfortable Russian Jews, the United States was, by far, the preferred destination. Yet, the American immigration system's Russian quota was completely full and so it was not an option within the foreseeable future. Australia was also a possibility, but then it was a far-off and unknown country and sponsors were required. Few of us knew anybody who could serve as a sponsor. Then Canada became a serious possibility, as there were rumours that the Canadian government was actively seeking immigrants. Our family rushed at that option, and, surprisingly, at first, this avenue seemed promising. We were overjoyed, as we saw Canada as a backdoor means of eventually getting into the United States. So, the plan was that as soon as Father sorted out our affairs with the Chinese authorities, we would go to Canada. Unfortunately, the bird was only in the bush, not in the hand. We let our hopes rule our assumptions.

With Alex Vinogradov just before his departure, 1951

19

PLANNING THE FUTURE

*'When you arrive, write me a nice long letter, with all
the details of procedure on arriving in Australia.'*
Letter from Sam to Alex Vinogradov, 1951

By June 1950, I had successfully completed my first year at St Francis Xavier's College and I was promoted to complete the final year. The new Chinese authorities informed the Marist Brothers that the next scholastic year would be the school's last, as in September 1951 the school would be taken over as a Chinese state educational institution. This had already happened to all of the Chinese schools around us and during our classes we could hear the students in the school across the road singing the new communist national anthem and other patriotic songs.

St Xavier's, like most other schools of its type, prepared its students to sit the entrance examinations for one of the well-known English, French or US universities. With a written acceptance into Cambridge University in England, we would also possess a wide choice of other universities to enter. The British consulate in Shanghai served as a venue for sitting the exams. The answers were then sealed, under consular supervision, and shipped to England for marking. The problem was that by then, the consulate had virtually closed down and the university no longer offered the entrance examinations in China.

The students at St Xavier's and other schools were thus left high and dry, as we could no longer have our final year of education internationally accredited. Without the foreign university entry certificate, who would accept the results of the final examination of a school in China? I don't know what the other schools did, but the Brothers hit upon a brilliant solution. They were prepared to assure all of the institutions we would be applying to, that the final examinations would be in May-June (1951) as per usual and that they would be set in line with the Cambridge University entrance examination standards. They promised to mark our exams based on their many years of experience with this procedure. It was hoped that these assurances would be accepted, due to the reputation of the school and the school's extensive international networks in the tertiary arena.

Our destination was to be Canada, and Brother Jules Raphael, the principal, had a contact at a Jesuit university in Quebec, Laval University, who agreed to accept me to study Chemistry, then my preferred choice. The only problem was that it was a French university, but it was no time to be choosy and I immersed myself in my studies to ensure that I would achieve the requisite marks. A private French tutor was employed to improve my language skills and I ended up doing very well in my exams. I even topped Catechism of all things. I received a special honour from the Roman Catholic Bishop of Shanghai, including the privilege of kissing the ring on his finger at the final prize-giving ceremony of the school. My parents were annoyed that their Jewish son achieved this result. After the ceremony, Father said, 'Why couldn't you have done that well in Mathematics?' The Brothers also gave me the prestigious task of delivering the valedictory address on behalf of the students. Speech night was an emotional occasion, for we all knew that our school, which had been operating without interruption since 1874, would close down, probably forever.

Then disaster struck. The Canadian government, with many apologies, reneged on the issuing of our entry visas. Apparently the immigration pressure from many Chinese fleeing the communist regime was so great, that the government felt unable to commit to a timeframe for us. Others were similarly affected. It was a terrible blow as we were under considerable pressure to hasten our departure from Shanghai. To me, this setback was particularly acute, as I was hoping to reach Quebec by the beginning of the academic year in September 1951. All these plans were put on hold until another solution could be found. Our morale was low as the uncertainty of our position weighed heavily on us all.

Meanwhile, the communist authorities were pressing Father to turn over the factory, without compensation. Then ownership of the other four properties was put in question, as private ownership of real estate property was being abolished in favour of state ownership. Selling the properties was not an option, as all the possible buyers had simply melted away.

We became totally preoccupied with the task of finding a destination for our resettlement. Until then, Australia had been only a very distant possibility. But Eva, in desperation, remembered that a distant relative from her side of the family was living in Melbourne, Australia. I was unaware that Eva had remained in contact with her family. With pressure mounting daily, she got hold of this relative's address and explained our plight, effectively asking him to sponsor our family, sight unseen. It was miraculous that this letter actually arrived at its destination. The Korean War was in full swing and communist China had cast its lot with the North Koreans, who were supported by the Soviet Union, against the United Nations, led by the United States, Britain and Australia. All correspondence was by airmail, via Hong Kong, then still a British Crown colony.

The relative in question, Grischa Sklovsky, agreed to provide the sponsorship papers. As a sponsor he had to guarantee to the Australian government that we, the Moshinsky family, would not be a financial charge on that government. Whilst Father was able to assure him that we possessed the necessary funds to look after ourselves in Australia, the final responsibility was still legally his. We did not even know then whether Grischa's personal financial circumstances permitted him to provide that assurance.

Later, we realised what a courageous and compassionate act it had been. Grischa's family had once been quite affluent in Siberia, but in Australia he was not a wealthy man. Before the war, Grischa had left Siberia and gone to Europe. While studying Chemistry in Lyons, France, he met and fell in love with an Australian woman, Celia Weigall. During the war, Grischa served in the British army. Tragically, he lost his mother and sister during the Holocaust. At the end of the war, Grischa and Celia were reunited, married and settled in Melbourne, where Celia's family was based. Celia was from an Anglo-Saxon milieu as far removed from that of European Jewry, as it is possible to imagine. The Weigalls were well established in Melbourne and her father held the prestigious position of president of the medical association. Grischa, however, had a modest job, a mortgage, a daughter, Anna, and plans to have more children. Whilst it was not clear at that time, in retrospect, as much credit is due to Celia, as to Grischa, for agreeing to sponsor our family.

As I got to know her, I realised that she had been fully supportive of Grischa's decision to respond to Eva's plea in such a truly humanitarian way.

We were overjoyed when we received news that they would sponsor us. We were determined to have our application for an Australian visa processed as quickly as possible before anything could go wrong. Mr Gill, an official of the British consulate, was assigned to our case on behalf of the Australian government's immigration department. He was under enormous pressure, as he was responsible for processing many other families who, by now, were all urgently seeking to leave Shanghai. A basic condition of entry to Australia was good health, so each of us had to undergo a variety of health tests, particularly on our lungs, as tuberculosis was still a common ailment. Finally, Mr Gill issued us with the requisite visas and we could plan our departure.

In the meantime, Father's negotiations with the Chinese authorities continued at a snail's pace. This was very frustrating, as we couldn't obtain the requisite Chinese exit visas until all the property issues were resolved.

We then realised that my admission to a French-speaking Canadian university was pointless. As the Sklovskys lived in Melbourne, we assumed that we, too, would settle in Melbourne, although a number of our friends were settling in Sydney. So I wrote to the University of Melbourne, requesting admission and waited, with baited breath, for an answer. Soon we received, with a great sigh of relief, a favourable response. My admission to the University of Melbourne was accepted on the basis that I had already been accepted into a recognised university in Canada, 'subject to satisfaction that my English was of an adequate standard'.

Negotiations with the Chinese authorities stalled and my family was faced with a difficult decision. Finally, it was decided that I should make the journey to Australia ahead of the rest of the family. This would allow me to finalise my university entrance issues and, also, to make the necessary arrangements for the rest of the family for their eventual arrival.

This was a major step for a young man who grew up in a very sheltered environment, but my family was comforted in the knowledge that I would be accompanied by friends who were also leaving and who could look out for me during the journey.

How would I fend for myself upon arrival in Australia? Apart from the Sklovskys, we did not have any relations or close friends in Melbourne. The Vinogradovs were leaving shortly for Australia, but we did not feel we could impose upon them. So, another letter was sent to Grischa requesting that I be able to stay with them until the rest of the family arrived. He generously agreed to welcome me into their home. Speedy measures were taken to ensure an early departure that would have me in Australia before the start of the academic year in March 1952. We engaged a Chinese gentleman who understood the workings of the new bureaucracy. His job was to take me to all the authorities that needed to sanction my departure, so an exit visa could be granted. The problem was, because I was stateless, I didn't have a passport, so there was no document to which to attach a visa. Thankfully, the International Refugee Organisation was issuing documents specifically designed for this purpose.

Every morning, the Chinese gentleman took me all over Shanghai to meet with the relevant departments. There, we would lodge the appropriate documents, and then sit and wait patiently for an interview. During the interviews, my Chinese guide acted as my interpreter, as by then, Mandarin was the official language and I only spoke the Shanghai dialect. This process took up the whole morning, and, frustratingly, could not be continued in the afternoon. Finally, after two weeks, the authorities were satisfied I could leave China. This was relatively quick because I was only a boy, with no personal history of any business activities. Each department formally consented to my departure and affixed their stamp on to my United Nations travel document. Only after all the required stamps, or chops, as we called them, had been obtained, could an exit visa be issued and the travel bookings be made via the China National Travel Company, a state-run institution which controlled all travel arrangements in China.

The travel plans were complex, but made easier because I was travelling on my own. The key was to find a berth on a ship travelling from Hong Kong to Australia. The earliest available ship was a small cargo vessel, *The Anking*, scheduled to sail in early October for a three-week journey to Sydney. We were pleased that I could get to Sydney well before university started. But it was particularly challenging getting a reservation at a hotel in Hong Kong, as the city was full of refugees, all clamouring for accommodation, while waiting for their ship to depart. Eventually, friends of the family, the Godkins, who were living in Hong Kong, were able to book a room for me at a small hotel in Kowloon.

The months leading up to my departure were intense and stressful. I had to get rid of most of my possessions, as it was simply impossible to leave with everything I had accumulated. This was easier said than done. Shanghai was awash with personal belongings that everybody was leaving behind. The whole process was quite heart wrenching. Most of my things had to be virtually given away, as sellers were many and buyers were practically non-existent.

Admittedly, I did not make matters easy for myself. A few months earlier, I had purchased a 20 volume set of the Encyclopaedia Britannica from a hawker on Avenue Joffre. He charged me according to the weight of the entire set based on the prevailing price of scrap paper. It came to so little that I simply could not resist the bargain. I loaded it on to a pedicab, as rickshaws had been banned by the new authorities, and brought it home. I was thrilled with my purchase but Father was dismayed. When the decision was made that I would travel soon, Father delighted in ordering me to get rid of my 'damned encyclopaedia', as there was no way I could take it with me. So, I returned to the same hawker, with the same 20 volumes. He put them back on the scales and gave me a figure based on the new price of scrap paper. I can't recall what the difference was, but I had enjoyed owning it for that short time. I had particularly loved reading the sections on Canada and Australia.

Getting rid of the encyclopaedia was easy compared to my other possessions, for which I had hoped to get cash. We had to give away most of my books, comics and clothes. More troublesome were the chemicals and photographic papers which Alex and I had accumulated for our photography 'business', the Ascot Photo Studio. The Vinogradovs had left Shanghai very quickly and so I also had the unhappy tasks of organising for their cat to be put down and cleaning up Alex's room in the apartment below. The sense of distance was already apparent and I wrote to Alex to let him know that I was taking care of things after his hurried departure. Later, I would be grateful that Alex kept my letters.

Dear Vino (Alex)

I am writing you this letter just a day after you have left, as I would like to give you an account of what I did and I would also like to ask you some questions. To tell you the truth, I begin to miss you already, as the place doesn't seem to be the same without you around.... I immediately got down to work in cleaning your apartment. Really Vino, the amount of junk that there can be in a house.... I found several Australian pamphlets left on the floor. What should I do with them? They are a Handbook of Australia and two others. I also found a thick file of your father's correspondence. Do you want me to burn them? What shall I do with the hundreds of pics and negatives I found? ...

Say Vino, I have a really big favour to ask of you. When you arrive, write me a nice long letter, of all the details of procedure on arriving in Australia. About the ship etc. I hope you know what I mean. You see I am leaving alone at the beginning of October for Melbourne. Any advice is welcome. Thanks.

I remain your best pal,
Sammy

I also wrote to Alex about the parties. We were all teenagers by then and keen on dancing and jiving to the latest American music. 'Dancing Cheek to Cheek' was a popular song, but it was also a way of dancing that was new and exciting. We wanted to develop steady girlfriends, but what was the point? Everyone was leaving. It began to dawn on us that we would never see our close friends again. Not only were we saying goodbye, but it was for good. As our numbers dwindled, normal cultural differences were abandoned and everybody was invited to the parties, Catholics, Protestants, Jews, Chinese and Europeans. We were in the midst of our teens and we were beginning to feel sexually liberated. We drank a lot more alcohol and we got into the spirit of creating 'cool' cocktails. We weren't concerned about drink driving, as most of us went home by pedicab.

In my last year in Shanghai, I discovered the joy of reading. The number of comic books I read after the war distressed my parents, and they used to restrict how many I was allowed to devour each day. But virtually overnight, my comic book obsession disappeared. In the well-stocked library of the Jewish Club, I happened to pick up a book by Somerset Maugham, and I started reading it. The book was *Of Human Bondage* and I recall the excitement of becoming totally immersed in it. From then on, while waiting for my exit visa, all my free time was spent reading in the library.

During this period, Grandmother and I talked a lot; she imparted her accumulated lessons on life and her instinctive wisdom. She was dreading my pending departure and being left on her own. She still missed Grandfather very much; they had been a close couple, in mind and temperament. She was not close to her only son, my father. Over the years she had confided in me that she was disappointed in him. Basically, she did not respect his judgement or his personality. Abe was a very considerate person and a great father to me, but he was not the powerful personality that his own father had been, and it was immensely difficult for him growing up in Grandfather's shadow. Father was not a courageous decision-maker and he found it difficult to make the timely decision to sell our Shanghai assets and to relocate us elsewhere. One day, when we were sitting on the balcony, Father confessed to me that he was terrified about how he would manage in a totally new and different country. Grandmother always felt that Grandfather would have pulled off our departure from Shanghai far more successfully.

Towards the end of August, I was notified that my Australian visa had finally come through, subject to medical fitness, including a cardiogram test. We then realised that the Chinese exit visa application showed Canada as my destination. The bureaucrat handling this matter was not pleased and caused a further frustrating delay. This period was fraught with anxiety and anticipation. On the 24th August, when I finally got an appointment to see Dr Smolnikoff to have a heart test, I was so excited that my heart rate was too high, so he sent me away to calm down. After a few days, I did pass the medical tests and my Australian visa finally came through on the 28th August 1951. A few days later, the change in the exit visa was approved. Finally I was free to leave Shanghai.

Above: New Years Eve 1950-1951
Below: A farewell party

Another
farewell party

On a hike in Victoria, 1952

20

FIRST IMPRESSIONS

'There is little new under the sun.
Beware of false new things.'
Miriam Moshinsky

I arrived in Canton by late evening. After a three-day rail journey, it was a welcome relief. All the foreign train passengers were ensconced in a large hotel, and after settling in we had a late dinner together. Our freedom to move around the city was restricted, but we had to be up early anyway for the final leg of our journey, the short train trip to Sum Chon, on the border with Hong Kong.

As soon as I got on the Hong Kong-bound train, I sensed a totally different atmosphere, of freedom and plenty. Hong Kong was still very much a British Crown colony and all the things we missed in Shanghai were available in abundance. Eva's friends, the Godkins, who were in the travel business, met me at the Kowloon terminus and drove me to the Grand Hotel, where I would stay for a week before boarding the ship to Australia. The hotel was small, but clean and comfortable and centrally located near a number of air-conditioned cinemas showing American films.

An important job I had to do while in Hong Kong, was to pay a visit to the leading bank, The Hong Kong and Shanghai Bank. I had to present Father's instructions to issue me with an Australian currency draft. I was ushered into an office and treated with deference; they called me 'mister' and served me a cup of tea. After much checking and signing I ended up with an impressive-looking document addressed to The Bank Of New South Wales (now Westpac Bank) authorising it to hand over 1,000 Australian pounds to me upon its presentation. I left the bank feeling more adult and a step closer to Australia.

Finally, *The Anking* was ready to board passengers for the voyage to Sydney. It was essentially a cargo vessel, with minimal passenger facilities. It was scheduled to make stops at Ocean Island and Nauru Island, two specks in the Pacific. There were about 30 passengers and our individual accommodation was sparse but clean. We took our meals together and the atmosphere, after a few days, became friendly and comfortable. Fortunately there was a good variety of food.

The passengers were a mixed lot, nearly all of whom were making new homes in Australia. Naturally, the conversation turned to our uncertain future. There was however, one Australian, a wool buyer named McNamara, who was returning home from a business trip in the East. He was a very entertaining fellow and enlivened the journey. He tried to introduce us to the essentials of our new life in Australia. First there was 'two-up', which he told us was essential to our integration, much to the consternation of many of the older passengers. Then there were the horse races, which he told us all Australians indulged in, the results of which he managed to tap into via the ship's radio. To us, the idea of horse racing was associated with the very elitist Shanghai racing scene. His crowning achievement was to organise a 'sweep' for the approaching Caulfield Cup in Melbourne. One of the passengers, a German, drew what must have been the favourite horse. McNamara offered him double what he had put in and the poor fellow was in a quandary for a few days over whether to take up the offer. The prospect of doubling his investment, no matter how small, before setting foot into Australia was enticing indeed. He pestered everybody to help him make a decision. Eventually, he took up the offer. The horse won and he missed out on a larger sum.

Finally, on the evening of the 24th October 1951, we entered Sydney Harbour. It was already quite dark and so, apart from the myriad of lights, we missed out on the city's magnificent panorama. At the pier, I was met by the Vinogradovs and a very excited Alex. Also there were the Prostermans, together with their daughter Lily. They were friends of the family who had rented an apartment in the Doumer Apartments for a few months prior to their own departure for Australia. Eva had arranged for me to stay with them for a few days before catching the train to Melbourne. Despite the relief of seeing friendly faces, I recall feeling a deep anxiety now that the reality of starting life in a new land took shape. I began to understand the emotions of a refugee, the giving up of a familiar life for an unknown future.

Nevertheless, those first few days in Sydney were a great introduction to Australia as Alex was so keen to infect me with his own enthusiasm. We travelled everywhere by public transport and remarked that there were literally no Chinese about, no rickshaws, no pedicabs and no beggars. And everything was in English. We visited the Harbour Bridge and Bondi

Beach and marvelled at the endless number of single dwellings with gardens. Everybody told me how lucky I was to go to Melbourne, as the Melbourne Cup race would shortly take place. Unfortunately, it was not possible for me to telephone my parents to describe my experiences, I could only send a brief telegram to advise that I had arrived safely and that all was well.

After a few days, it was time for me to take the train to Melbourne. I phoned Grischa Sklovsky and he told me what day was convenient for him to meet me. Alex took me to Central Station and I purchased a ticket. It was all so exciting to do this without Chinese intermediaries and without having to show documents and visas.

My train arrived at Spencer Street Station and Grischa was there to meet me and take me to his home in his little Fiat. On the way, passing through the city, I remarked how empty it was, with most of the shops closed. It was Melbourne Cup day, everybody was at the races.

The Sklovsky residence was in Camberwell. It was an old timber home, spacious and with a large and beautiful garden. Celia, holding a crying little girl, Anna, who was recovering from measles, welcomed me. They showed me to the room that would be my home in Australia until the arrival of the rest of the family. I could not have wished for a more inviting beginning.

That evening, as we sat down for dinner in the kitchen, I realised that this was a very different country. Celia herself had cooked the dinner, serving what she considered a delicacy. It was a rabbit, in a stew, no less. I felt too old to cry and too polite to reject it. I was in a total panic, but I somehow survived the ordeal. Certainly, Grandfather would not have given me a job in his factory based on how I ate the rabbit stew. After dinner came another eye-opener. Grischa asked me to help him clean up the kitchen while Celia put Anna to bed. I was taken aback when he went on to tell me that he would wash the dishes and I would dry, but that I should watch closely, as next time, it would be my turn to do the washing up.

The following Sunday morning, after breakfast, Grischa took me out into the garden and said that the lawn had to be mowed with a hand mower. I gasped in disbelief. After demonstrating to me how this had to be done, he left me to it. That evening, he announced that as it was Sunday night, the rubbish tins had to be taken out. There were no wheeled bins then, nor was any of the rubbish separated. So the rubbish tins were heavy and had to be lifted out into the street. It certainly was an exhausting week, full of totally new personal experiences. But I found the routine to be a wholesome change from the type of life I had led in Shanghai.

By the time I left Shanghai, with the ordeals and upheavals of the final years, I had become sick and tired of being a foreigner, no matter how comfortable life was. I was more than ready to be an integral part of a new society and I really embraced Australia. I warmed to the evident equality of the individual, the overall atmosphere of honesty and importantly, the tolerance I encountered. I felt that at long last, fate had intervened to our advantage. I couldn't wait to share my enthusiasm for this new country with the rest of my family. Our hopes for a secure and fulfilling existence seemed within reach.

Grischa and Celia Sklovsky with
Anna, Jane and Michael, 1959

UNITED NATIONS

IRO

International Refugee Organization
Far East Mission

CERTIFICATE OF TRAVEL

No. B-671

The United Nations International Refugee Organization requests all civil and
military authorities of Foreign States to let pass freely Mr. Abraham MOSHINSKY
bona-fide refugee, eligible for IRO assistance, going to ~~ISRAEL~~ --AUSTRALIA--
under the sponsorship of IRO, and afford assistance in case of necessity.

Joseph Liao
Acting Chief
for G. Findlay Andrew,
~~Director,~~ Chief
~~Shanghai Branch Office~~
IRO. Far East

Place of Birth: Odessa, Russia
~~Nationality:~~
Date of birth: 14 August 1904
Height: 5' 10"
Weight: 175 lbs.
Colour of eyes: Grey
Colour of hair: Blonde
Special peculiarities: -------

Accompanied by:
(Only Dependents under 16 years):

....
                                                          (Relationship)   Age

Issued at: Shanghai, China
Date: 5 April 1950
Expiration: 4 April 1951
Renewed until: 3 April 1952

EPILOGUE

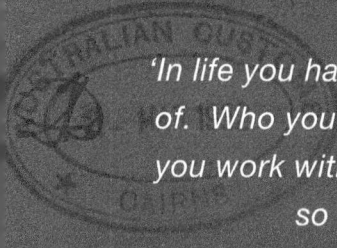

'In life you have three important things to take care of. Who you marry, who your friends are and who you work with. Over the rest you have no control, so pray that you will be lucky.'

Miriam Moshinsky

Father, Eva, Nathan, Elijah and Grandmother finally managed to extricate themselves from Shanghai and made the same journey that I had made the previous year. They arrived in Sydney on the 8th March 1952, on the passenger vessel *Changsha*. I had booked them into a hotel on Bondi Beach and flew up to Sydney to meet them.

It was a joyful reunion, for there had been moments when I was concerned that our separation would be more protracted. I had been particularly worried about whether Grandmother would be able to make the arduous journey to Hong Kong and survive the long sea voyage.

Father wanted to stay in Sydney for several days to catch up with a number of friends who had settled there. The large majority of those from Shanghai settled in Sydney, the first port of call. I took him around to see them and he gathered information on how best to make a start in Australia. While most were optimistic about future prospects, they all counselled that doing business in Australia was very different from Shanghai. There were still shortages lingering from the war, and there were no Chinese compradors to pave the way ahead.

I had lived at the Sklovskys the whole time since arriving in Melbourne. Grischa had been determined to give me a crash course on how to integrate into the Australian way of life. I think he was appalled by how useless I was. So he had got me a job in a service station and also sent me on a long hitchhiking trip. My biggest initial problem, however, was to obtain accommodation for the rest of the family in Melbourne. This was no easy matter as there was still a severe housing shortage. Celia Sklovsky was very helpful and eventually I was able to rent a modest home that, fortunately, was also in Camberwell, not far from the Sklovskys.

By the time I met the family in Sydney, I felt reasonably seasoned in the weird and wonderful ways of Australia. I escorted them to Melbourne and we settled into the rented house in Allambie Avenue. The first thing we had to get used to was the outside toilet. The silence, particularly at night, of a Camberwell street in the early 1950s was, at first, eerie and unsettling. The Sklovsky family offered their advice and assistance. The neighbours around us appeared mildly curious, but displayed courtesy and friendliness.

The brunt of the initial difficulties fell upon Eva and she rose to the challenge. There was no cook or amah and, from the start, the shopping had to be done and the family had to be fed. Celia helped out by 'lending' us her cleaning woman, until we could organise our own. There was so much to be done in a short time. Nathan and Elijah had to be enrolled in the local state schools and we had to learn how to move around on public transport, as Father had not yet bought a car.

About a month after the family had more or less settled in came Pesach and we had to organise our first Seder in a new country. Every aspect of this was a new challenge. Where to get the matzos, the gefilte fish and all the other foods? Fortunately, I had brought a Haggadah from Shanghai with me. It was not until we sat down, the six of us, that we realised how alone we really were. Apart from Grischa, who did not participate in religious ceremonies, we did not know anybody. There was nobody to invite and nobody to invite us. Many years later, with a large and growing family, it brings me great joy to see so many family members sitting around the Seder table together. The loneliness of that first Seder in Melbourne will always haunt me and underline how fortunate we are now.

On Father's shoulders fell the daunting task of providing for a family in a new country, where business conditions were altogether different to those he was used to in Shanghai. Having arrived with some capital, he felt that he ought to emulate his own father and go into business, which was probably not the right thing to do. Unfortunately he did not have any luck with his various business ventures. But this did not dent his optimism about the future. He and Eva ensured that the normality and happiness of our family life was not affected and that my brothers and I continued to focus on our education.

To this day I miss my father very much. I will always remember him as a warm and gregarious individual and a wonderful father. Unfortunately he was robbed of seeing the success his sons would eventually enjoy. He died suddenly after collapsing from a brain hemorrhage on Saturday the 16th November 1963.

Grandmother had to endure the tragedy of seeing her own son buried. Despite her disappointment in Father during his lifetime, at his funeral, her grief showed that she was, above all else, a devoted mother. She lived at home with us until a fall necessitated her being admitted to The Montefiore Home, where she would receive the attention she required. Throughout all the years, we remained very close. We talked often, in Russian, as she never mastered Chinese or English. She was a very perceptive woman, unbelievably so considering her age and her background. As I completed my studies and started in the professional world, she took me aside one day and gave me the benefit of her observations. She said to me that in every society and grouping of people, even among the 'joulikies' (crooks in Russian) there is always the need for one honest and trustworthy person in the middle, whom all sides value and respect. She said that I should always strive to play that role. I have, and this advice has always stood me in good stead.

When Ada and I were seriously contemplating marriage, I brought her to The Montefiore Home to see Grandmother, where I acted as translator. It was not a long meeting, but Grandmother got the measure of Ada, enough to tell me a few days later that she was happy to give us her blessings. As the courtship progressed, Grandmother asked me one day what Ada proposed to do after marriage. She knew from our first meeting that Ada was studying law. I said perhaps she would give up her studies when she had a husband. Grandmother told me that under no circumstances should I allow this to happen. She said that I should ensure that Ada finish her studies, start a career and earn money in her own right. She said that only when a wife has her independence and self-respect does the marriage remain strong. I followed her advice, literally rewriting Ada's lecture notes, as her handwriting was so illegible that even she could not decipher them. How proud Grandmother would have been to witness Ada's successful career in law and the family we raised together. Grandmother died on the 31st July 1967, aged 81. Fortunately, Mark was born shortly before her death and one of my most cherished photographs is one of her holding him, with me alongside. She was very special to me and I feel so fortunate that she was such an important part of my life. She continues to inspire Ada and me to play a meaningful role as grandparents to our eight grandchildren.

Eva continued to live in Melbourne for a number of years while Nathan and Elijah were completing their education. The difficult years in Australia, with the many problems Father experienced, took their toll on her spirit. Eva and her sister Nusia continued to be very close and cared for each other very much. After Nusia's husband Boris died, Nusia asked Eva to join her in Sydney and Eva readily accepted. Nathan and Elijah had both married and were pursuing their careers and her life in Melbourne had become increasingly lonely as her friends passed away. Those years in Sydney were reasonably happy for them. They socialised with their many friends from Shanghai who had settled there. Unfortunately, Nusia contracted dementia and Eva had to have her put into a special care hostel. She visited Nusia every day, even though Nusia could not recognise her. Eventually, Eva developed cancer and when she deteriorated we had to bring her back to Melbourne under special care at The Montefiore Home, where she died on the 14th October 1999, aged 87. I will always be grateful to Eva for giving me so much affection and ensuring that I enjoyed a stable family life.

As the years passed, the difference in age between Nathan, Elijah and myself became less significant and we got to know each other in a way that had not been possible in Shanghai. There, they were still babies as far as I was concerned, and we only really saw each other at family gatherings. But we were raised to look upon each other as brothers rather than half brothers and we are now close, just as Father and Eva would have wished it. They have both raised lovely families and carved out successful careers – Nathan as a Queens Counsel and Elijah as an opera, theatre and film director of international renown.

And now to Alex. The Vinogradovs settled in Sydney on arrival in Australia and Alex lived with them while pursuing his studies at the institution that became the University of New South Wales. We would often see each other on holidays, either in Melbourne or in Sydney. He pursued a technical career while I gravitated to the financial field. Despite this and the geographical separation, we remained the closest of friends. We would spend hours in conversation, reminiscing on a level that only true friends can enjoy. Fortunately, marriage to Barbara and career eventually brought him to Melbourne, which made it much easier for us to sustain our close and unique relationship.

On the 21st September 1986, I experienced a severe pain in my chest. I went to bed and Ada called our doctor, who gave me a sedative. While I was asleep, Barbara rang to inform us that Alex had passed away from heart failure, while visiting his ageing parents in Sydney. I was devastated to lose a close friend whom I had known for nearly half a century. With his passing, I felt, both physically and emotionally, that a Shanghai part of me had also died.

We maintained contact with the Sklovsky family, always inviting Grischa and Celia to significant family gatherings. Occasionally, Grischa felt the urge to reconnect with his Russian roots, so he would drop in for a meal of herring, potatoes and a dose of vodka. I looked forward to our chats and hearing about his children Anna, Michael and Jane. Grischa died on the 8th January 1995, aged 80. Celia survived him for another nine years, eventually passing away on the 19th May 2004, at the age of 89. In her will, Celia asked me to act as executor and I was pleased to carry out this function. To me, it was a fitting way to personally express my gratitude for their kindness and faith in our family so many years ago.

I never heard from my mother again. The meeting in the park was the last time I saw her. I later learnt that she had gone to the United States at the end of the war. Whether she attempted to contact me to say goodbye, I do not recall. She was not at my Barmitzvah, nor did I hear from her on that occasion. She stopped being part of my life. Only curiosity would have propelled me to find her and make contact with her. I felt that would entail a price I was not prepared to bear, as it would have been hurtful to both Grandmother and Eva. I was concerned that they would interpret any search as a sign that I was not totally happy. This may seem heartless, but I feel that I acted honestly and with sensitivity to those who really mattered to me.

Over three generations, my family tried to establish roots. From the oppressive tsarist Ukraine, to remote Vladivostok and then Shanghai, despite initial promise, our attempts to create a permanent home were not successful. There always seemed to be a force at work that propelled us to move on. But the Moshinsky family has now been in Melbourne, Australia, for over half a century and two new generations have come into existence. Here, I am optimistic that we can continue to thrive, nourished by our religious culture and the richness and diversity of our past.

With Grandmother
holding Mark, 1965

The Bund, 2006

When I left Shanghai in October 1951, amidst the enormous changes being wrought by the new communist authorities, I was sure that it was a definite 'farewell' rather than the more hopeful 'au revoir'.

Over the next 35 years, despite the preoccupations of education, work, marrying and raising a family, I tried to follow events in my former home. This was not easy, for under Chairman Mao, China again reverted to being a closed society. Foreigners had departed, few visited and information out of it was carefully filtered. I read about initiatives with grandiose names, like 'Great Leap Forward' and 'Let a Thousand Flowers Bloom', but I remained unaware of the turmoil within Chinese society which they caused.

Whilst Ada and our three Melbourne-born sons, Mark, Randall and Richard, were fascinated by my stories of Shanghai, thoughts of travelling there seemed outside the realm of possibility. Still, I never lost hope.

And then in September 1976, aged 83, Mao Tse Tung died of natural causes. The world watched closely, eager to know how the succession process would actually work out in the authoritarian regime he had established and controlled so closely. Despite some initial confusion, the transition took place without bloodshed. In 1978, the diminutive Deng Xiaoping, a senior member of Mao's early team, but later a victim of the disastrous Cultural Revolution, assumed control. Shortly afterwards, he set about reversing many of the excesses of Mao's regime, including the opening up of China to the world. By 1986, travel to China, and Shanghai in particular, became permissible, on a very controlled basis. So, in June of that year, we travelled as a family to China and Japan.

I was very excited to return to Shanghai and to introduce my family to my eastern origins. I didn't know what to expect and I was stunned by how little Shanghai had changed physically. With the exception of a few new hotels, the city appeared to have been frozen in time. I was able to show them the scenes of my early life, just as they looked then. Our guide knew nothing about the former life of the city, so he graciously let me take over the tour.

In many other respects, the changes were substantial, much of it for the better. The reforms I witnessed before I left had continued. The abject poverty, which I grew up alongside, had disappeared. Prostitutes no longer roamed the streets nor were there any beggars. Opium dens, the bane of Chinese life, had been banished and the more humane pedicab, a bicycle drawn vehicle, had replaced the rickshaws.

Also gone, however, was the colour and elegance for which Shanghai had been famous. A cloud of drabness and decay seemed to envelop the city. Nearly everyone wore the ubiquitous Mao uniform of blue grey baggy pants and jacket. Sadly, the once opulent and majestic buildings looked neglected and dreary with washing hanging out of the windows. The few people we met seemed welcoming, but apprehensive.

We started off at the factory on Rue Lafayette. The facade had changed very little from when I last saw it. It was still carrying on the business of printing and was renamed a 'people's factory', but it was no longer making ice cream cups or elaborate chocolate boxes. All the old machinery was still there, completely intact, as was Grandfather's desk, still in exactly the same position. It was exciting to be able to sit at the desk, just as I had done as a boy. The staff were friendly but totally bemused by our visit. Unfortunately, the apartment above the factory was off-limits as it had been turned into a storage area.

We then walked around the familiar streets and through the French Park. We were allowed a very quick pass through the Ecole Municipale, which had been turned into a scientific institution. Walking along Avenue Joffre was a great disappointment, as this once elegant shopping boulevard no longer offered any exciting merchandise nor any of its former glamour.

The following day, we travelled to Rue Doumer, which had its name changed to Donghu Lu just before I left Shanghai. The short street still retained its appeal because of the lovely plane trees lining it. We easily found the lane leading to the Doumer Apartments but initially we were not permitted to enter. It had been turned into a furnished apartment establishment for visiting officials and the few foreign businessmen who came to Shanghai. After some explaining, we were allowed in. The entrance area looked unkempt. Grandfather would have been very upset to see its state, as he was fastidious about appearances. The apartment I lived in was off-limits as it was rented out, however the one next door was being renovated and we entered. Despite its emptiness, it was nowhere near as spacious as I had remembered. The once lovely garden in front of the building was also neglected.

Opposite, the Doumer Cinema, the venue of so many hours of enjoyable film viewing, was still standing, but was closed. St Joan of Arc's down the street was intact and we were, surprisingly, allowed to walk through and look at one of my classrooms. The buildings and the spacious grounds were much as I remembered them. The tuck shop cart was, however, gone.

We then crossed Avenue Joffre and entered Rue Pichon, where the Jewish Club had been located. It was easy to find and now housed the conservatorium of music. Here again, we were free to enter and wander about and I could show everyone the club building, particularly the large room in the front where my Barmitzvah lunch took place. The Betar building was also still standing.

We walked around the corner to Route Tenant de La Tour to see if the synagogue was still there. Fortunately it was, but barely. The basic structure was as I remembered it, but it had been converted into a warehouse. The only vestiges of the past were the outlines marking where the three Stars of David used to be. The best way for us to get a good overall view of the building was from a position standing across the road. While there, I noticed a man with a woman and two young boys in front of its entrance and he was clearly trying to explain something to them. On an impulse I decided to cross the road and tap him on the shoulder. I wanted to tell him that the building once housed the synagogue of Shanghai's Russian Jewish community. As he turned around, I immediately recognised him as Arik Joffick, the son of our family doctor. He was living in England and had also decided to show his family his roots in Shanghai at the first possible opportunity. We laughed at the coincidence.

The next day, our last one in Shanghai, I decided that we should visit the Bund. The walk along the Bund was heart wrenching for me. The buildings were all there but they were terribly run down, many of them had Chinese people literally camping in the once majestic entrances. Judging by how the facades had deteriorated, there was really no point in even trying to go inside. So we took a lunch cruise on the Whampoo River, crowded with sampans, and I explained to Ada and the boys how once this section was full of American and British warships.

In the afternoon we had our guide take us to St Xavier's and it was still there, functioning as a school. Outwardly it had changed little and, surprisingly, we were welcomed in once our guide explained the purpose of our visit. A senior member of the staff came down and appeared genuinely pleased to see me. He was happy to show us around and I was again able to visit my old classroom, where nothing had changed. The Chemistry and Physics laboratories, where Alex Vinogradov and I had spent so much time, were also there, unchanged. In the schoolyard, Richard joined some of the students in a basketball game, just as I had done 35 years earlier. It was a fitting way to end our visit.

I don't think my sons were very impressed with the Shanghai of 1986. In fact they said to me that they were pleased that the communists had taken over the city and forced the foreigners out. I expressed surprise, as the takeover resulted in my family losing so much. They replied, if the communists hadn't forced you out, we might have had to grow up in this place!

It would be another eleven years before I had the opportunity to re-visit Shanghai. By 1997, Deng Xiaoping's reforms had gathered considerable momentum and the city was regaining its former commercial prominence. This time, just Ada and I went for a few days. We stayed at a luxurious hotel, one of several which had recently been built. We visited the newly opened Shanghai Jewish Museum, housed on the top floor of the original Russian Jewish synagogue, built in Hongkew in 1928. Nanking Road and Avenue Joffre had shed their drabness and again had become a mecca for up-market shoppers. The New Synagogue had been turned into a restaurant and we ate at a table right near where Father's seat had once been.

On this trip I visited Professor Pan Guang, whom I met a year earlier in Melbourne, when he opened an exhibition on Shanghai Jews at the Jewish Museum of Australia. Professor Pan is the dean of the Centre for Jewish Studies at the Shanghai Academy of Social Sciences, a body dedicated to the study of the Jewish experience in Shanghai and China. As a boy he grew up in the French Concession and was intrigued by the Russian Jews he had met and befriended. He and his centre have brought alive to visitors the unusual Jewish experience in Shanghai.

It was a most satisfying visit. I was so pleased to see the city of my childhood being revitalised and attempting to take its place among the great commercial and cosmopolitan centres of the world.

When we went back again in September 2004, we enjoyed a most exciting visit. Early in 2004, I received an invitation to participate in celebrations commemorating the 130th anniversary of the founding of St Francis Xavier's College. The reunion was organised by a former classmate, Denis Alonso, a resident of Los Angeles. The celebrations were held at the school site in Hongkew. Much of it was built over with tall new buildings, but the original school itself was intact, minus the imposing statue of Jesus. There were about 20 ex-students, spanning a number of years, including a number of spouses, who managed to make the celebrations. The ex-students were welcomed with genuine warmth and much generosity across lunches and dinners over several days. The tenor of these celebrations underlined the desire to link the present school, named the Beihong High School, to the old St Xavier's and to draw a link between the two schools operating out of the same premises.

It was wonderful to meet up again with Denis Alonso and to compare notes on our experiences since leaving school and Shanghai. The master of ceremonies of the events to welcome us back was Mario Machado, whom I first met at the Shanghai American School. Of course, I missed Alex Vinogradov very much. We had often talked, in Melbourne, of making a return trip together. Unfortunately none of the Marist Brothers, our wonderful teachers, were there. We were told that they had either passed away or were too old to travel. The reunion was, nevertheless, a great opportunity to reminisce about old friends and happy days gone by.

This visit to Shanghai was memorable for a number of other reasons. Prior to our departure from Melbourne, on the suggestion of a friend, I made contact with Tess Johnston, a former American diplomat now living in Shanghai. When I called her on the telephone, I found out that she was living in the very same apartment in the Doumer Apartments in which I had lived. In fact, she was talking to me from the balcony where Grandmother and I had spent so much time together. Tess is a lover of and expert in art deco. She also has a passionate interest in Jewish history and culture. She settled in Shanghai because of its many art deco buildings and diverse Jewish heritage. It was great to meet her in my old apartment.

Our trip also coincided with Rosh Hashanah, the Jewish New Year, and on that day I went to the new Jewish Centre, run by Rabbi Greenberg. It was, for me, a very moving experience. The last time I prayed in Shanghai was over half a century earlier in the synagogue on Route Tenant de la Tour, just before it closed down.

Finally, I was able to look into the status of the properties that we had left behind. Fortunately, our buildings (two in the French Concession and two in Hongkew) are still standing, though the worse for wear and tear due to lack of maintenance. Through the good offices of Sam Gerovitch, the respected consul general of Australia in Shanghai, who was also born there, we were able to have a meeting with the Chinese authorities, who updated me on the situation. Unfortunately, there seems to be little prospect of their return to us in the near future.

Our most recent visit was in May 2007. When Ada mentioned to a number of friends and relatives that we were going to Shanghai, we were inundated with people wishing to join us. Everyone saw this as an opportunity to get a personal tour of old Shanghai by me. I ended up as the tour leader for a dozen friends including two sets of in-laws, Estelle and Stan Fookes and Emma and Henryk Kranz.

It was a special and nostalgic treat for me to show them Shanghai. Thanks to Tess Johnston, we all walked through my old apartment in the Doumer Apartments. Then I was able to show them all the areas of my childhood, which they had heard so much about, including Avenue Joffre, the former Jewish Club and what remained of the synagogue, which had recently been damaged by a fire.

Shanghai seemed to have totally reverted to its former glittering self. The shops were laden with goods, the restaurants were full and at night the city was aglow with bright lights. Many of the grand buildings along the Bund had been restored and it was even possible to enter them to view the magnificent public areas.

For me, a highlight was the side trip to Moganshan with Emma and Henryk, and Irene Pletka, who also grew up in Shanghai. Moganshan had only recently been opened up to tourism. We walked a lot, up and down mountain trails, and I reminisced about that happy summer in 1948. Fortunately, I brought with me some of the photographs from our stay and they helped our guide to find the waterfall, a major tourist attraction then and now. We also located what I believe is the solid stone villa that our family had rented.

I am so glad that I was able to revisit Shanghai on these four occasions. Each had its own highlights for me, reinforcing my feelings of warmth for Shanghai the wonderful city in which I was privileged to grow up.

1. The terrace houses for the key factory workers.
2. Sam in his former classroom at St Francis Xavier's College.
3. The Shanghai Jewish School, now Shanghai Education Department.
4. With Brother Gilbert, former principal of St Joan of Arc's College in Paris, June 1991 (see endnotes - chapter 13).
5. With Mark, Randall and Richard in the yard of the Doumer Apartments.
6. With Arik Joffick outside the Russian Jewish synagogue.
7. Outside the new wing of St Joan of Arc's College.
8. The Russian Jewish Synagogue, originally The New Synagogue.
9. Sam's classroom at St Joan of Arc's College.
10. St Francis Xavier's College.
11. With Ada and sons in a pavilion in the old walled city of Shanghai.
12. Outside the Doumer Cinema.
13. The family at a Chinese restaurant in Shanghai.
14. Sam's tour group, 2007.
15. Standing beside the same desk that Grandfather and Father used in the Shanghai Cardboard Box Factory.
16. Richard in the grounds of the Shanghai Jewish Club.
17. At the St Francis Xavier's College reunion in 2004.

FORMER NAME	CURRENT NAME
Route Pere Robert	Ruijin Lu
Rue Lafayette	Fuxing Zhong Lu
Bund	Zhongshan Dong Lu
Rue Doumer	Donghu Lu
French (Koukaza) Park	Fuxing Gongyuan
Avenue Joffre	Huaihai Zhonglu
Nanking Road	Nanjing Lu
Avenue Petain	Hengshan Xilu
Rue Pichon	Fenyang Lu
Seymour Road	North Shaanxi Lu
Route Tenant de la Tour	South Xiangyang Lu

ENDNOTES

CHAPTER ONE

1. *North China Daily News:* this newspaper was the leading English language paper of Shanghai and I remember my father reading it every day. It principally addressed the Anglo-Saxon trading elite and it was modelled on *The Times* of London, then the paragon of the English-speaking world's newspapers. Like *The Times*, its front page consisted of classified advertisements, while news and events followed in the later pages. I was able to obtain a copy dated the 3rd July 1934 and I have used it to provide a snapshot of life in Shanghai and the world into which I was born.

CHAPTER TWO

1. My grandmother is named in a number of documents as Maria Davidovna, a Russian naming convention suggesting that her father's first name was David. Her maiden name was Caisman and she was born in Odessa on the 25th December 1886.

2. The rich Jewish life of Odessa was immortalised in the colourful *Odessa Tales* by Isaac Babel.

3. *Pale of Settlement:* this term was given to a region of Imperial Russia along its western border, in which Jews were allowed to permanently reside. Beyond this region, Jewish residence was generally prohibited. Tsar Catherine the Great established the Pale of Settlement in 1791.

4. A number of Jewish conscripts deserted the Russian Army and some of them, serving in the east, made their way to Shanghai.

5. *Shtetl:* a Yiddish term denoting a small town with a large Jewish population, in pre-Holocaust Eastern Europe. There were many shtetls in the Pale of Settlement.

6. *The Kishinev Pogrom*: this was an anti-Jewish riot or massacre that started after an incident on the 3rd April 1903, when a Christian Russian boy was found murdered and the Jews were (incorrectly) blamed. The riot spanned three days, over which time 47 Jews were killed, 97 were severely wounded and over 700 houses were looted and destroyed.

7. The American Jewish community is largely made up of Jews from Russia and Poland who fled persecution. My grandmother's family, the Caismans were settled in Chicago. Father visited them in the 1920s and again in 1947. I met them in 1960 when I worked in Chicago.

8. *The Intervention:* the name given to the action of American President Woodrow Wilson, who, in July 1918, deployed US troops to join other allied forces in Russia.

Although the public reason given for this mission was to safeguard tsarist military supplies and the Trans-Siberian Railroad, the true purpose was to topple the new Bolshevik regime. Some of the American troops were also stationed in Vladivostok. The action was a failure and all the troops involved were eventually withdrawn.

9. A number of people have provided assistance and information to improve the quality of the historical background in this chapter. I was extremely lucky to be introduced to Dr Elena Govor through Ella Goldberg. Dr Govor specialises in Russian-Australian contact and has written widely on the subject. She suggested to me that there could be a mine of information on my grandparents in Vladivostok and she first found Grandfather's name mentioned as one of the founders honoured when the Vladivostok synagogue was returned to the Jewish community. Dr Govor then provided contacts in Vladivostok who were prepared to undertake research on my behalf. In June 2008, I was fortunate to visit Vladivostok with Ada. Upon arrival, Professor Galina Kanevskaya steered me through the State Archive of the Territory of Primorye, where we found mention of my grandfather's arrival in Vladivostok. Slava Savruev, a director of the Gorky Drama Theatre of Vladivostok, located the houses owned by my grandparents from photographs I had sent him. We were then able to see the houses and meet a resident. Slava was also able to find a reference to my grandfather's factory in an old Vladivostok business directory. Professor Larissa Vitaljevna was also helpful in filling in some historical gaps regarding the days before Vladivostok became fully part of the Soviet Union. Rabbi Yisroel Silberstein, Chief Rabbi of Vladivostok and the Primorsky Region, was especially welcoming. My arrival in Vladivostok coincided with the unveiling of an ambitious plan to renovate a number of synagogues in Russia which had been handed over to local communities by the new Russian government. The fact that a grandson of one of the original founders of his synagogue was arriving proved very exciting for the Rabbi and his wife Aliza. They were both extremely hospitable and generous with their time. While there, I also met Mr Grigori Klebanov, the community's president and Sasha Kuzmin, who was researching the early days of the synagogue. They managed to unearth some interesting early documents that also mentioned my grandfather and his involvement in the affairs of the synagogue. Our visit to Vladivostok was unforgettable. Walking through the streets of a city that is only now beginning to experience architectural change, and visiting the homes of my grandparents, was like resurrecting the ghosts of past lives.

CHAPTER THREE

1. For a complete account of the Opium Wars, see the engrossing book *The Opium Wars – The Addiction of One Empire and the Corruption of Another* (see resources).

2. The Yangtze River is one of the great rivers of the world. It runs over 6,000 kms and to the Chinese it is known as Chang Jiang, meaning Long River. It virtually bisects China into two and over 500 million people live, work and trade along its banks.

3. During the American Revolution in 1776, Spain, a foe of the British, sided with the rebellious colonists. It was then the principal source of silver and refused to supply it to the British.

4. The French had negotiated a separate treaty with the Chinese in 1844, giving them their own territory, which they named 'The French Concession'.

5. The Chinese administered areas were in the old walled city, in Nantao, Chapei (in the north) and in Pootung, on the other side of the Whampoo River.

6. *Termination of extraterritoriality:* during November and December of 1943, the American and British leaders met in Cairo on their way to the Teheran Conference with Stalin. On the 1st December, they issued what is known as the Cairo Declaration, a promise to the Chinese under Chiang Kai Shek, to return Manchuria, Taiwan, and the Pescadores Islands to Chinese sovereignty following the defeat of Japan. In addition, they agreed to abolish the terms of the Treaty of Nanking, the pre-war system of extraterritoriality whereby Chinese courts had no jurisdiction over any foreigner residing in China. As a result, the various foreign settlements and concessions would cease to exist.

7. *Ashkenazi Jews:* the descendants of the medieval Jewish communities of the Rhineland, West Germany, who also migrated eastward from the 10th-19th centuries. They developed a distinct culture and liturgy influenced by interaction with the surrounding peoples, including a unique language, Yiddish. The term derives from the medieval Hebrew word, 'Ashkenaze' for Germany.

CHAPTER FOUR

1. The Instrument of Divorce was only registered with the Shanghai Ashkenazi Communal Association, which was a reflection of the prevailing practice whereby each community acted as a registrar of its own affairs.

2. The terms of the divorce were amended on the 28th July 1936 and notarised by the Jewish communal officers.

3. Whether my full head of hair at 75 years is a reflection of these annual shavings I do not know. I will give my grandmother the benefit of the doubt.

4. The term 'amah' is peculiar to the east and originates from several sources: the Portuguese 'ama' meaning nurse; the Medieval Latin 'amma' or mother; and there is possibly a Hebrew connection in 'imma', also meaning mother. An amah is a female servant engaged in a wide range of domestic duties. In prosperous families with young children, amahs were extensively used for looking after children. Sometimes amahs were also wet nurses.

CHAPTER FIVE

1. Some Kaifeng residents claim to be Jewish and steps are being taken to bring them back to the faith, but this can be only be achieved through re-conversion. For, in line with the practice of their Chinese neighbours, the few remaining Kaifeng Jews adopted patrilineal descent as the basis of their identity. As a result, they cannot be recognised as Jews in the orthodox rabbinical sense where matrilineal descent prevails.

2. The Emperor was called Henry Pu Yi. He was immortalised in the film, *The Last Emperor.*

3. China had agreed, in 1896, for Russia to build a railroad across Manchuria right up to Vladivostok. By then, Japan's aggressive designs in the region were feared and this railroad was part of a wider treaty of mutual cooperation between Russia and China. Harbin became a key hub of this gigantic project and many Russian Jews gravitated to the city because of the economic opportunities.

CHAPTER SIX

1. The Ecole Municipale was established in 1926 by the ruling authorities of the French Concession, primarily to cater to the children of the growing number of French people living in Shanghai.

2. Bastille Day falls on the 14th July, commemorating the beginning of the French Revolution in 1789.

3. One of the soldiers in the Polish Army was my father-in-law, Mietek Gringlas.

4. The Public Thomas and Hanbury School (PTH) was the premier English language school in Shanghai. It was the result of the 1931 merger of two established British schools; the Shanghai Public School and the Thomas Hanbury School. Its culture was very English. The sports curriculum included cricket (played in the Racecourse grounds) and rowing (on Soochow Creek). It did not discriminate against Jews

as its students included a number of boys from the leading Sephardi families. In 1941 when Japan declared war on Great Britain and the US and occupied the International Settlement, the school was taken over by the Japanese and was closed down.

CHAPTER SEVEN

1. The late J.G.Ballard describes the Japanese interment camps in his novel *Empire Of The Sun* which was adapted into a film produced by Steven Spielberg.

2. Japan's decision not to attack the Soviet Union was conveyed by its master spy in Tokyo, Richard Sorge. It was a godsend to the Soviets who had suffered immense losses at the hands of the German army. As a result, it was able to deploy a substantial number of Siberian troops to its war on the western front.

CHAPTER EIGHT

1. *Sephardi:* this word means 'from Spain', which in Hebrew is Sepharad. In the Jewish context the term is applied to the descendants of the once numerous communities that thrived during the Muslim rule in Spain. Although not equal in rights and standing to the Moslem inhabitants, over 400 years the Jews in Spain did not suffer persecution and many reached high office as advisers to the Muslim rulers. That period is also been called 'The Golden Years' because of the vibrant Jewish cultural life and relative freedoms that were allowed to exist. The Jews of Spain originally came from Baghdad and other places in the Near East where there were old established communities, following the paths of Mohammedan conquests. As they settled in these countries, they imported the rabbis and traditions from Baghdad. Following the Christian conquest of Spain by Ferdinand and Isabella, those Jews who refused the mandatory conversion to Christianity were expelled in 1492. They now comprise an extensive network of Jews who fled to the Arab world carrying their religious traditions with them. In the case of the Sephardi Jews of Shanghai, it should be noted that they never originated from Spain, but from Baghdad from where a number migrated to India.

2. Harbin was the capital and the largest city of Manchuria. It grew with the arrival of the Chinese Far Eastern Railway which drew a lot of Russians, including Jews. Harbin became a haven for those escaping the Bolshevik revolution. In fact, it once contained the largest Russian population of any city outside Russia. It also had a very vibrant Russian Jewish community.

3. Betar is the Revisionist Zionist Youth Movement founded in 1923 in Riga, Latvia, by Vladimir Jabotinsky. The name stands for Brit Josef Trumpeldor, a Jewish fighter who fell defending the settlement of Tel Hai from an armed Arab group.

CHAPTER NINE

1. Kristallnacht, which owes its name to the countless shards of glass that lined the streets in the wake of violent anti-Jewish demonstrations throughout Germany and Austria, took place on the 9th November 1938. The wanton destruction of Jewish property and synagogues was instigated by the Nazi Storm Troopers and Hitler Youth as retribution for the shooting of a German diplomat in Paris by a young Jew, Herschel Grynszpan. He had been enraged by the plight of his parents following their expulsion by the Nazi authorities from their homes in East Germany. Following the events of Kristallnacht, anti-Jewish measures were stepped up to force Jews to leave Germany and Austria. This precipitated considerable determination by the remaining Jews to seek safety anywhere. In due course some 18,000 Jews arrived in distant Shanghai, one of the havens available to them.

2. The final group of Jews to arrive in Shanghai from August-October 1941 were the mainly religious Jews from Kobe, in Japan. Their remarkable story of flight and survival is documented in M.Tokayer & M.Swartz's *The Fugu Plan. The Untold Story of the Japanese and the Jews during World War II.*

CHAPTER TEN

1. *Rickshaw*: a mode of human-powered transport where a runner pulls a two-wheeled cart seating one or two persons. The word originates from the Japanese word 'jinrikisha' which literally means human powered vehicle. It is a form of transport that was prevalent in Asia, originally for the social elite. In Shanghai rickshaws were as common as taxis in a large city and were very cheap to use. My father had his own rickshaw which was much cleaner than most and took him around wherever and whenever he needed. Following the takeover of Shanghai by the communist forces in 1949, rickshaws were banned in favour of the pedicab where the puller sits on a bicycle.

2. *Kapparot*: an ancient Jewish custom where a person's sins are believed to be transferred to a live chicken swung over the head. The chicken is then slaughtered and its meat, or an equivalent amount of money, is given to charity. A rabbinical comment on this practice says that witnessing the bird's death should evoke an awareness of the fragility of life, leading to a spirit of repentance.

3. *Pesach or Passover*: a Jewish holy festival marking the escape of the Hebrews from their enslavement in Egypt. During the eight-day period, unleavened bread or matzos, is eaten instead of bread.

4. *Seder*: a Jewish ritual feast and dinner held on the first and second nights of Pesach, at which family and friends participate. The primary purpose of these gatherings is to read the Haggadah, which is an account of the exodus from Egypt.

5. *Afikoman*: a half piece of matzos that is hidden in the early stages of the Passover Seder. At most Seders the children find the afikoman and return it for a reward from the person conducting the Seder.

6. *Manishtana*: in Hebrew means 'what has changed' or 'why is this night different to all others'. It is the first line of a song referred to as 'The Four Questions', which is sung by the youngest child at the Pesach Seder table.

CHAPTER ELEVEN

1. *Minyan*: the name for a quorum required for certain Jewish religious obligations. Traditionally it consists of ten adult men, although some liberal strands of Judaism accept adult women in making up a minyan. It is often referred to the services held for the seven (or less) days following the death of a Jewish person.

2. *Shiva*: this is part of a series of Jewish customs for bereavement. It is the week long period of grief and mourning for the close relatives of the deceased, involving the cessation of most regular activity - hence the term 'sitting shiva'.

3. *Kaddish*: one of the most important and central prayers of Jewish liturgy, now mostly used in referring to the prayer recited at funerals and memorials.

4. *Yahrzeit*: a commemoration of the death of a Jew by a mourner, usually a child, sibling or parent. Its date is calculated according to the Hebrew calendar, being the anniversary of the death (not the burial) of the loved one. The Kaddish (see 3) is recited on these days.

CHAPTER TWELVE

1. The B-29 derives from the Boeing B-29 Superfortress, a four-engine, propeller-driven heavy bomber flown by the US Air Force in World War Two. It was designed as a high altitude bomber and was the primary aircraft used in the bombing of Japanese cities.

2. *Pao Chia*: the name given to the self-policing units established in 1942 by the Japanese in Shanghai. It comprised of all foreign and Chinese men aged 20 to 45.

3. *Hirohihito*: the name of the Emperor of Japan who announced the surrender of his country on the 15th August 1945. He was the 124th emperor, reigning from 1926 to his death in 1989, aged 88. After the War he cooperated in the remaking of Japanese society.

CHAPTER THIRTEEN

1. *The Cold War*: the name given to the acrimonious relationship that developed between the United States and the Soviet Union following the end of the Second

World War. Although allies in the war to defeat Nazi Germany, pre-war ideological differences and distrust surfaced after victory. The Cold War dominated international politics, right up to the collapse of the Soviet Union in 1991. The relationship got its name because both sides were afraid of going to war against each other, fearing that the nuclear weapons possessed by each side could destroy the entire world.

2. St Jeanne d'Arc College was founded in Shanghai in1920 as an annex to the Aurora University (the French-run Jesuit University) for the children of foreign residents who wanted to study French. In 1922, the Marist Brothers took over the running of the school and a new building was established at 18 Rue Doumer on the corner of Avenue Joffre. The French section closed down in 1950 and the English section was taken over by the Communist authorities in 1953.

3. In late June 1991, I had the wonderful experience of meeting up with Brother Gilbert, the principal of St Jeanne d'Arc College when I was a student there. Ada and I were in Paris and I decided to see if there was an entry for the Marist Brothers in the telephone book. There was, so I rang and asked if there was anybody there from Shanghai. I was told that a Brother Gilbert was living there who may have been from China. He wasn't in and so I left my name and a message that I would call back. I spent the rest of the day anxiously wondering if it could really be the same Brother. Amazingly, when I called back, it was him and he remembered me clearly! When we met, he had all the class photos ready to show me. We spent hours reminiscing. It was such a joy for me to meet up with him again a few days later and to be able to introduce him to Ada as well as Mark and Sidra, who had just arrived.

CHAPTER FOURTEEN

1. Kuomintang (KMT) was established in 1905 as China's Nationalist Party. It became the vehicle for converting China from a feudal empire to a republic. Dr Sun Yat-sen, the founder of modern China, became its President in 1921. It was China's dominant political party until 1949, when it was overthrown by the Chinese Communist Party (which was also founded in 1921, in Shanghai).

2. Chiang Kai-Shek (1887-1975) was a Statesman and General. He took over control over the KMT in 1927 as a vehicle for ruling China. He became a symbol of China's resistance to Japan's aggression. He was an opponent of Mao Tse Tung and the Communist Party and lost the civil war against it in 1949. He fled to Taiwan as a result.

CHAPTER FIFTEEN

1. *Barmitzvah*: literally means 'son of commandment' and determines the responsibilities of a Jewish adult. According to traditional Jewish law, every Jewish boy becomes a Barmitzvah at the age of thirteen and thus becomes obligated to follow the commandments. In addition, he becomes eligible to be counted in a prayer quorum (minyan), lead prayer services and testify before a religious court. With those belonging to Liberal or Progressive Judaism, the Barmitzvah rights and obligations are extended to girls when they turn twelve or thirteen.

2. *Parasha*: the section of the Torah applicable to the relevant Sabbath, read by the Barmitzvah boy (or girl) called to bless and read the Torah.

3. *Haphtarah:* a series of selections from the books of the Prophets that is publicly read in the synagogue as part of Jewish religious practice. It is read following the appropriate Torah portion and is thematically linked to it.

4. *Kiddush*: a blessing recited over the wine. It is also the light ceremonial meal served at synagogue at the end of the service.

5. *Bima*: meaning 'high place' is the elevated platform on which the Torah is read.

6. *Horah*: a traditional Jewish dance in a circle that has long been used as a medium for the expression of joy and other communal emotions.

7. *Hatikvah*: a song whose words evoke the age-old Jewish hope for the re-establishment of a sovereign and free Jewish state. Following the establishment of Israel in 1948, this song was adopted as its national anthem.

CHAPTER SIXTEEN

1. Moganshan is a mountain top village built by missionaries and other foreigners in the early 1900s as a summer retreat. It is about 200 km from Shanghai and its cool temperatures, in contrast to Shanghai's humid summer heat, made it a favourite getaway. After 1949, it was called the East China Sanatorium, a peoples' health resort. It is gradually reverting to its role as a retreat on summer weekends. Many of its now run-down facilities are being refurbished.

2. *Coolies*: a term denoting manual labourers, particularly from China and India. It was often used derogatively during the European colonisation of Asia to describe people in low status work.

CHAPTER SEVENTEEN

1. Mao Tse Tung (1893-1976) was the leader of the Chinese Communist Party. He was present at its first congress in Shanghai in 1921. He led the epic 'Long March' and founded the People's Republic of China in 1949. He initiated a number

of reforms, some of which, including 'The Great Leap Forward' and 'The Cultural Revolution' turned out to be disastrous. But many reforms were positive. For example, the banishment of opium smoking and other vestiges of imperial and foreign rule, were of lasting benefit.

2. *HMS Amethyst*: a frigate of the Royal Navy which was the subject of an incident on the 20th April 1949 while sailing the Yangtze River from Shanghai to Nanking. She came under sustained fire from the communist forces on the northern banks of the river, sustaining extensive damage and losing 22 sailors. To us in Shanghai, the fact that a Chinese force was able to fire with impunity on a British warship, was a telling sign of how the balance of power had changed in our world.

CHAPTER EIGHTEEN

1. St Francis Xavier's College was established on the 21st September 1874. It was one of the first Catholic schools in Shanghai and it catered to the fast growing foreign community. From small beginnings, the school grew rapidly and in1884, moved to the Hongkew district. The Marist Brothers took over the running of the school from the Jesuit founders and ensured that the school maintained its reputation as one the leading schools in China. When the communist authorities took over the school, it was renamed Bei Hong High School. The new school administration maintained its reputation as an elite school and acknowledged its origins. To that end, I attended a reunion in 2004 marking the school's 130th anniversary.

RETURN TO SHANGHAI

1. *Bund*: an Indian term meaning 'embankment along a waterway'. The Shanghai Bund, built alongside the Whangpoo River, a tributary of the Yangtze River, is probably the world's most famous embankment. Most of Shanghai's prestigious buildings were built along the Bund including the Cathay (now Peace) Hotel, the Shanghai Club, Customs House, the vast Hong Kong & Shanghai Bank and the British Consulate. The buildings along the Bund define Shanghai's well-known skyline.

RESOURCES

Ballard, J.G. *Miracles of Life, Shanghai to Shepparton, An Autobiography.* Fourth Estate, London.

Barber, Noel. *The Fall of Shanghai. The Communist Takeover of 1949.* Macmillan London Limited.

Brossollet, Guy. *Les Francais de Shanghai 1849-1949.* Belin, Paris.

Cohen, J. *The Jews of China.* Gesher Volume 3 No. 5 September 2008.

Collar, Hugh. *Captive in Shanghai. A Story of Internment in World War II.* Oxford University Press, Oxford, New York.

Eber, Irene. *Voices from Shanghai. Jewish Exiles in Wartime China.* University of Chicago Press, Chicago & London.

Eisfelder, Horst. *Chinese Exile. My years in Shanghai and Nanking.* Makor Jewish Community Library, Melbourne.

Finnane, Antonia. *Far From Where? Jewish Journeys from Shanghai to Australia.* Melbourne University Press, Melbourne.

Hanes, W.Travis (III) & Sanello, Frank. *The Opium Wars. The Addiction of One Empire and the Corruption of Another.* Robson Books, London.

Kranzler, David. *Japanese, Nazis and the Jews. The Jewish Refugee Community of Shanghai. 1938-1945.* Solomon Rabinowitz Hebrew Bookstore, New York.

Krasno, Rena. *Strangers Always. A Jewish Family in Wartime Shanghai.* Pacific View Press, California.

Liberman, Yaacov. *My China. Jewish Life in the Orient, 1900-1950.* Gefen Publishing House, Jerusalem.

Lin Yutang. *The Wisdom of China. An Anthology.* Michael Joseph LTI, London.

Professor Pan Guang. *The Jews in Shanghai.* Shanghai Pictorial Publishing House, Shanghai.

Ristaino, Marcia Reynders. *Port of Last Resort. The Diaspora Communities Of Shanghai.* Stanford University Press. Stanford, California.

Ross, James R. *Escape to Shanghai. A Jewish Community in China.* The Free Press (Macmillan, Inc), New York.

Sergeant, Harriet. *Shanghai, Collision Point of Cultures, 1918-1939.* Crown Publishers, Inc. New York.

Spence, Jonathan & Chin, Annping. *The Chinese Century - A Photographic History.* HarperCollins, London.

Tokayer, Marvin & Swartz, Mary. *The Fugu Plan. The Untold Story of the Japanese and the Jews during World War II.* Gefen Publishing House. Jerusalem.

Tata, Sam & McLachlan, Ian. *Shanghai, 1949 The End of an Era (Photographs and Introductory Text).* B.T Batsford Ltd, London.

Willett, Robert L. *Russian Sideshow. America's Undeclared War, 1918-20.* Brassey's Inc. Washington D.C.

Websites

www.english.migdal.ru

www.jstor.org

www.shtetlinks.jewishgen.org

www.jewishencyclopedia.com

www.wikipedia.org

www.history.com

www.virtualshanghai.ish-lyon.cnrs.fr

AUTHOR'S ACKNOWLEDGEMENTS

This memoir has enabled me to indulge in my love of history. I am indebted to and thank the authors of the texts, articles and websites I have consulted.

I am very grateful to my daughter-in-law Romy Moshinsky for editing and publishing this memoir. She applied herself to the difficult process with much effort and expertise. She brought designer Jacki Starr into the team and she fully embraced her enthusiasm for the project. I could not be more pleased with the result.

For their considerable assistance with my research in Vladivostok, I thank Dr Elena Govor, Professor Galina Kanevskaya, Professor Larissa Vitaljevna, Mr Grigori Klebanov and Sasha Kuzmin. I am also grateful to Rabbi Yisroel Silberstein, Chief Rabbi of Vladivostok & the Primorsky Region and his wife Aliza for their hospitality.

Two residents of Shanghai were both encouraging and helpful - Professor Pan Guang, Dean of the Centre For Jewish Studies at the Shanghai Academy of Social Sciences and Tess Johnston, who graciously allowed us to visit the Doumer Apartments and generously shared her unique knowledge of Shanghai. I am also grateful to her for sending me the postcard of Nanking Road.

Here in Melbourne, Horst Eisfelder has imparted his great knowledge of Shanghai, particularly the experiences of the Central European refugees in Hongkew, where he lived during the war. Our frequent chats have been of enormous assistance. Rachel Konig was also very kind in giving me permission to include a photograph taken in Hongkew by her father Stefan Konig. Thank you also to Tony Withers for giving me old postcards of Shanghai including the ones of the Shanghai Racecourse.

Special thanks to Barbara Vinogradov, who generously gave me all the letters that I wrote to Alex over the years. I would also like to mention two close friends, Rabbi Dr John Levi and Leon Silver, who are both successful authors. They gave me encouragement together with a lot useful advice based on their own experiences.

This memoir is the result of incredible support and assistance from my family. Thank you to my daughters-in-law, Sidra and Natalie and also Mark who reviewed the manuscript. Their sense of perspective and command of language was very helpful. I want to make special mention of my wife Ada. Together with my sons Mark, Randall and Richard, she has continuously encouraged me to write about my early life. Her unwavering support has been invaluable.

www.ingramcontent.com/pod-product-compliance
Lightning Source LLC
Chambersburg PA
CBHW051850090426

42811CB00034B/2286/J